SCRATCH COOKING 2

Revised Edition

by Benita McCoy Lyons

"IT'S THE REAL M^CCOY."

The Real McCoy, Inc.
3337 Rushing Wind Lane
Lexington, Kentucky 40511
or realmccoy05@windstream.net
www.kentuckyscratchcooking.com

ISBN 978-0-615-13900-5

Published by It's The Real McCoy, Inc.
Designed by The Serif Group. Printed by BookMasters, Inc.

Scratch Cooking was originally published
in 1989 by Benita McCoy Lyons,
It's the Real McCoy, Inc.

TABLE OF CONTENTS

BENITA IS A REAL MCCOY

Benita McCoy Lyons is a fourth generation descendant of the Hatfield–McCoy feud of American folklore, but she'd rather feed a Hatfield than shoot one these days.

The Hatfields and McCoys came together in the 1970s in front of the cameras of CBS News and officially ended their feud. The Kentucky McCoys and the West Virginia Hatfields now live in peace in the Tug River valley on the Kentucky–West Virginia border. The Winchester rifle that fired the feud's last shot is now Benita's treasured family heirloom after being displayed in the Smithsonian.

Benita would be happy these days if everyone who knows about the famous feud also knew the rich culinary tradition of her native Appalachia.

She is the founder, 100% owner and guiding force behind "It's the Real McCoy, Inc."—a company based in Lexington, Kentucky, that markets her cookbook, catering, and cooking classes.

Benita learned the recipes from her McCoy ancestors. Recipes in her "Scratch Cooking" cookbooks name their sources, so readers learn to make "Florene's Fresh Apple Cake." "Aunt Loretta's Corn Pudding" and "Idy Mae's Sour Dough Bread."

Her excellence has been recognized by the Kentucky Department of Agriculture, which certified Benita as an official Kentucky Food Producer whose products are good enough to bear the Kentucky Proud label.

We hope the enclosed materials help you understand Benita's feelings for the uniquely beautiful Appalachian culture, of which she and the famous feud are only small parts.

Those who would unjustly stereotype mountain people are failing to see the subtle beauty of eastern Kentucky life. Benita evokes this beauty in her foods, and wants to spread the good word about Appalachian scratch cooking because "It's the Real McCoy".

THE STORY OF THE FEUD

This is a true and factual story about my family heritage, the great vendetta of the Hatfields and the McCoys.

These two families were once friends and neighbors living in the Appalachian Mountains in a region known as the Tug River Valley. The Hatfields lived in Southern West Virginia and the McCoys in Eastern Kentucky. Although the Tug River separated them, it wasn't enough to keep their hate and vengeance toward each other apart, for during the Civil War their loyalties for their country caused a division that would never again bring the peace to their hearts that was once shared.

William Anderson Hatfield, who acquired the name "Devil Anse" during the war by holding off a company of armed men on a mountaintop called the Devils Backbone, was the leader of the Hatfield Clan. Randolf McCoy, better known as Randall, was the leader of the McCoys. These family chieftains were much alike—honest, family loving men.

After the war, Harmon McCoy, a brother to Randall was found murdered in a cave near a Hatfield cabin. Randall blamed Devil Anse for his brother's death, because Anse had shot and wounded Harmon during the war. Harmon had made threats towards Devil Anse but had not lived to carry them out. For this, Randall carried a grudge and would start the bad blood between the two that cost many their lives. Some say over 150 people were killed and that the feud lasted 20 years or more.

Peace had existed for a few years until the day Randall, while visiting his brother-in-law—a Hatfield—claimed ownership of a razorback hog. This incident went to trial, for so did a Hatfield claim possession. Six Hatfields and six McCoys were elected as jury, but one McCoy named Selkerk voted for the Hatfield side and the McCoys lost the trial. Randall was enraged and vowed revenge. At this point, there was so much fury built between the two men that pride would take its deadly toll over one razorback hog.

Many skirmishes occurred during the next few years. Bodies would be found in the woods, but never a witness and never a trial. One body found was that of Bill Staton, who had testified for the Hatfields as an eyewitness during the hog trial.

Election Day, August of 1880.
The Hatfields, although residents of West Virginia, dominated several voting precincts in Pike County, Kentucky. It was on that day that Johnsie Hatfield first saw Rose Anne McCoy.

Johnsie, the son of Devil Anse, and Rose Anne, daughter to Randall, fell in love that day. They put behind them the fact that their families were feuding and hated each other. Rose Anne went home with Johnsie and although Devil Anse took special delight in the fact that his bitter enemy's daughter was living in his house, he refused the lovers permission to marry.

After a year and several months, Rose Anne left the Hatfield cabin and moved to live with her aunt in Stringtown, Kentucky. Even though Rose Anne no longer lived with Johnsie, their love affair continued. Johnsie frequently visited Rose Anne. One night after hearing of Johnsie's visits, Rose Anne's brothers laid waiting and captured Johnsie. Rose Anne borrowed a horse from a friend and rode hard to warn Devil Anse of his son's capture. This proved to Devil Anse that Rose Anne loved his son. For the rest of his life he would regret not granting them permission to marry.

Rose Anne had no previous knowledge of her brothers' plans, but Johnsie blamed her and would never again cross the river to see her.

Rose Anne at this time was with child. She gave birth to a daughter, Sarah Elizabeth. At age 8 months, the baby died. Still with thoughts of betrayal, Johnsie stayed away. Soon Rose Anne lost the will to live herself. But she lived long enough to hear of the marriage of her lover to her cousin Nancy McCoy.

Another election day came and again the two clans were together, but this time the leaders were not present. Ellison Hatfield, a brother to Devil Anse, was there to head the Hatfields, and Tolbert McCoy, son of Randall, led the McCoys. A comment made by Ellison, which brought a roar of laughter, caused Tolbert to strike him directly in the stomach with a knife. The fighting broke out and Ellison Hatfield died from 26 knife wounds and one pistol shot. The three McCoys present, Tolbert, Phamer, and Randolf, Jr., were taken and locked in an abandoned schoolhouse for 24 hours. At approximately 2:00 p.m. the next day, they were tied to a tree and shot to death by the Hatfields.

Within 30 days of the slaying of the McCoys, the Pike County Grand Jury met and handed down 20 murder indictments. It would be several years before they were served and this brought the Governor of Kentucky, Simon Buckner into the feud.

Governor Buckner hired a lawman, Frank Phillips, to serve extradition papers on the Hatfields. However, under the leadership of Randall McCoy, he and Randall, led illegal raids into West Virginia killing any member of the Hatfield clan caught. This caused the Governor of West Virginia to get involved, for Governor Wilson and Devil Anse were close friends.

What had started as a family disagreement could have ended as a war between two states. The United States Supreme Court then intervened and put a stop to the argument between the two governors, but this action wasn't enough to stop the feuding because the illegal raids continued. Randall, at that time, had underestimated his enemy—for the Hatfields would not be defeated.

On January 1, 1888, Devil Anse and clan raided and burned the home of Randall McCoy, killing two of his children and brutally beating his wife. This episode caused Randall to move to Pikeville, Kentucky and Devil Anse to settle further into West Virginia in a town called Logan.

Randall had lost six of his children and not one of Devil Anse's immediate family had been killed due to the feud. Then, in the early 1890s, a bar brawl cost two of Anse's sons their lives. This weighed heavily on him and he then accepted the Lord Jesus Christ as his Savior and ended all of his fighting days.

People say that Randall had lost his mind over the deaths of his children and loss of his home. Though he was a broken old man, he stayed bitter and died that way.

Although many innocent people were involved in the feud by being either a Hatfield or a McCoy sympathizer, my short composition of this story is only to let the public know that pride, the backbone of a mountain man, can easily destroy if it gets out of hand.

Over the past 100 years and through several generations, peace has come to the valley of the Tug River. Industries, such as coal and lumber companies, have been built in the area and the idle time of the quiet mountain life has turned into a busy bustle.

My father, Leonard McCoy, is a direct descendent of the feud and was greatly interested in the roots of our heritage. He and his brother, Joseph, researched the story in the 1970s. They purchased a monument from a Hatfield for the McCoy gravesite, and for the public view, the Hatfields and McCoys officially buried the hatchet on CBS News.

Now, in the 21st century, the Hatfields and McCoys live together peacefully and happily ever after.

Benita McCoy Lyons

– 1 –

FAMOUS MOUNTAIN FOODS

NOTES

HILLBILLY HAMBURGER PIE

Grease casserole dish. In large skillet, brown 1 lb. ground round, drain. Add 1 chopped onion, 1 green pepper chopped, 3 tbsp. chili powder, 1 can whole kernel corn, drained, 1 can tomato soup. Pour into greased casserole dish.

Cornbread Mixture:
1 c. corn meal, ½ c. flour, 1 egg, 1 tbsp. Cooking oil, ½ c. buttermilk. Pour cornbread mixture over hamburger mixture. Bake at 350 to 400 degrees for 25 minutes, or until cornbread is done.

POTATOES AND SAUSAGE DISH

1 lb. Sausage, sliced and fried in 2 tbsp. fat
2 medium onions, chopped   ½ c. green pepper, chopped
1 clove garlic, minced   ½ c. red pepper, chopped
Salt to taste   Pepper to taste

Sauté the above vegetables
3 or 4 boiled potatoes, sliced
4 eggs beaten with 2 cups of milk added
Grated Swiss cheese

Layer all ingredients into baking dish and top with cheese. Bake at 350 degrees for 30 minutes.

MAMAW'S POTATO SALAD

Cook five medium potatoes, diced, until soft, drain.

Add 4 tablespoons corn relish, 1 medium onion, chopped, 1 tablespoon prepared mustard, 3 tablespoons mayo, 1 tablespoon sugar, 1 teaspoon salt. Mix all ingredients together and stir.

COCOA FUDGE

¼ cup cocoa   ½ cup corn syrup
¾ cup sugar   ½ cup milk
½ teaspoon salt   2 tablespoons butter
1 tablespoon corn starch   2 teaspoons vanilla

Combine dry ingredients in a saucepan, add corn syrup, milk and blend. Bring to a boil over medium heat stirring constantly. Boil 5 minutes. Remove from heat, stir in butter and vanilla. Cool without stirring. Place in well-greased glass casserole dish. Spread evenly & chill. Cut into squares or with a small biscuit cutter make rounds. (Also a small cookie cutter is good for children's parties.)

FRESH KALE

1 lb. Fresh kale, washed and stemmed
1 quart water   2 tbsp. Bacon grease
1 tsp. Vinegar   1 pat butter
Boil down hard until almost dry and kale is tender (about 40 minutes).

INDIAN CORN

Brown 1 lb. Ground round, drain. Dash salt and pepper to taste. Add 1 onion, chopped, 1 green pepper chopped, 1 can whole kernel corn, drained, 1 can stewed tomatoes, chopped and ½ c. ketchup. Simmer 20 minutes on low heat. Serve with mashed potatoes, green beans and corn bread.

MIMI'S MASHED POTATOES

6 medium potatoes, diced and peeled

2 c. water	1 stick butter
½ can evaporated milk	2 tsp. Salt
¼ tsp. Black pepper	

Bring potatoes to boil, cook until soft. Drain well. Place back in sauce pot, add 1 stick of butter, 2 tsp. Salt, ¼ tsp. black pepper, and ½ can evaporated milk. Whip with an electric mixer. Whip until fluffy. Serve immediately.

FLORENE'S FRESH APPLE CAKE

Batter:

1-¼ c. cooking oil	3 c. flour
2 c. sugar	3 c. peeled and chopped apples
3 eggs	1 c. nuts, any variety, chopped
1 tsp. baking soda	2 tsp. vanilla
1 tsp salt	

Blend oil and sugar well, sift dry ingredients, and add to oil and sugar mixture. Beat eggs slightly and add to batter; add vanilla. Fold in apples and nuts. Grease and flour a tube or bundt pan. Bake at 250 degrees for 1-½ hours.

Topping:

1 c. brown sugar	¼ c. evaporated milk
1 stick butter	1 tsp vanilla

Cook ingredients to a full boil. Beat and cool. Spread on cake.

RED TOMATO RELISH (SALSA)

12 ripe tomatoes, peeled and cored
6 large onions, chopped   6 green peppers, chopped
6 red peppers, chopped   3 banana peppers, chopped
2 c. sugar   3 c. vinegar (apple cider)

Stir all ingredients together and bring to a boil in a large cooker. Simmer for 45 minutes. Pour into clean dry jars, and cap with boiled lids. Seal.

**Served with tortilla chips, soup beans, and over orange roughy fish. To serve over orange roughy fish; pour salsa over fish and bake at 350 degrees for 30 minutes. You can add 2 cups chopped jalapeno peppers to make this salsa hot.

BUCKET STEAKS & GRAVY

6 minute steaks, washed and dried

Mix together 1 cup flour, 1 tbsp. seasoned salt, 1 tbsp. seasoned pepper, 1 tsp. garlic powder. Dip steaks in buttermilk and roll in flour mixture. Fry in 1 cup cooking oil until browned. Remove steaks from skillet, keep warm.

Gravy:
½ c. flour stirred into hot grease and meat drippings. Stir constantly over medium to high heat until brown. Pour in 2 cups cold milk slowly. Stirring constantly. Boil until thickened.

FRUIT COCKTAIL CAKE

Mix 2 cups flour
½ cup sugar
2 eggs

1 tsp. baking soda
½ tsp. salt

Pour into batter 1 #2 can fruit cocktail. Mix well and pour into ungreased pan, 9" x 13". Mix ½ cup chopped nuts and ½ cup brown sugar and sprinkle over batter. Bake at 350 degrees for 30 to 40 minutes. Melt 1 stick butter, 1 cup milk, 1 cup sugar. Let come to a boil and pour over warm cake.

MEAT LOAF

2 lbs. ground round
1 sm. can tomato paste
1 egg

1 c. bread crumbs
2 cloves garlic minced

Mix together with hands. Pat into loaf in greased casserole dish. Bake at 300 degrees for 30 minutes.

Sauce:
1 c. ketchup

1 c. light corn syrup (KARO)

Stir together and pour over meat loaf. Increase heat to 350 degrees and bake for 30 additional minutes.

BAKED BEEF ROAST

3 lb. chuck roast

2 c. water

Place in aluminum 9" x 13" cake pan. Pour in water. Season meat with seasoned salt and pepper to taste, garlic powder, 2 tbsp. A-1 sauce, ¼ c. Worcestershire sauce. Peel and quarter 2 large onions, 6 medium potatoes, 6 carrots. Place in oven, covered with foil. Bake at 350 degrees for 2 hours or until meat is tender.

SOUP BEANS

1 lb. pinto beans, looked, washed, and rinsed. Cover in sauce pot with warm water.
Wash and dry one Heavenly Ham bone or ½ lb. salt pork.

2 bay leaves, finely crushed   Pepper to taste
1 tbsp. sugar   Salt to taste
1 stick butter   1 tsp Mrs. Dash

Boil down hard for 20 minutes. Add 1 quart hot water. Simmer 4 hours. Stirring occasionally.

*Keep close check on water level; make sure water covers beans at all times.

SPICY BREAKFAST SPOONBREAD

3 c. milk
2 tsp. baking powder
1-¼ c. white or yellow cornmeal
8 oz. bulk breakfast sausage, cooked and crumbled
1 tsp. salt
2 tbsp. butter or margarine, melted
½ c. coarsely grated cheese
¼ tsp. pepper
¼ c. minced scallions
4 lg. eggs

Bring milk to a simmer over medium heat. Reduce heat to low and stir cornmeal in a fine steady stream. Stir in salt and cook about 5 minutes, stirring constantly until very thick. Stir in butter and pepper, taste, add more seasoning if desired. Cool 30 minutes until mixture is solid. Heat oven to 375°. Add eggs and baking powder to cornmeal mixture; beat thoroughly with electric mixer, gently fold in sausage, cheese and scallions. Pour into well buttered 2 qt. baking dish and level the surface. Bake 35–45 minutes until browned and puffy.

GREEN BEANS (FRESH)

2 lbs. fresh green beans, washed, broke and strung
1 tsp. seasoned salt   1 tsp. seasoned pepper
1 slab salt pork   Salt and pepper to taste
2 tbsp. cooking oil   Cover with water
1 tbsp. bacon drippings.

Boil down hard for 15 minutes. Reduce heat to low. Simmer for 45 minutes uncovered. Stirring occasionally. Check moisture, do not let cook dry.

GLAZED CARROTS

10 large carrots, peeled, sliced crosswise

Cook carrots in water until tender. Drain water. Add 1 stick butter and ½ cup honey, 1 tsp. cinnamon. Mix together and pour over carrots.

BEEFY OKRA

1 c. okra, chopped   1 c. onion, chopped
1 c. banana pepper, chopped

In a large skillet, mix these ingredients together and stir-fry in butter, garlic salt, seasoned salt and pepper. Add one can tomato sauce, one chopped tomato, and a dash of Italian seasoning to taste. Add to 1 lb. ground round, browned and drained. Simmer on low heat 20 minutes.

COLE SLAW

1 head cabbage   1 small onion
1 carrot   1 green pepper

Grate all ingredients in food processor. In small bowl mix together: 1 c mayo, 3 tbsp. lemon juice, 1 tbsp. Mrs. Dash, 1 tbsp. sugar, salt and pepper to taste. Stir together with cabbage mixture and chill before serving.

SAUCE FOR MEAT, ROASTS
(HARD TO COOK MEATS)

¼ c. oil   ¼ c. vinegar
¼ c. ketchup   1 tsp. garlic salt
1 tsp. dry mustard 1 tbsp. Worcestershire sauce
Rosemary to taste

Mix all ingredients together and pour over roast and bake according to roast directions.

SALMON PATTIES

2 cans pink salmon, drained and de-boned
1 egg
Salt and pepper to taste
1 c. crushed Zesta cracker crumbs

1 egg beaten
1 c. crushed Zesta cracker crumbs

Mix salmon, egg, salt and pepper, and cracker crumbs together. Roll into balls and then dip into beaten egg and then into cracker crumbs. Fry in 1 inch oil on medium heat until well browned.

The next four recipes were given to me by my Uncle Mix McCoy, the best potato fixer around these parts.

HOME STYLE POTATO CHIPS

Wash and dry 6 medium potatoes (do not peel). Slice thin. Deep fry in large skillet full of shortening until crispy golden brown.

POTATO STICKS

Peel 6 to 8 medium potatoes and shred finely. Add 1 c. sour cream, 1 c. grated cheddar cheese, ½ c. flour. Mix together and roll out into sticks. Roll in beaten egg and flour until coated and deep fry. Dip in homemade blue cheese dressing or cheese sauce.

FRIED POTATO SKINS

6-8 Hulls from baked potatoes. Deep fry hulls, as soon as removing hulls from deep fryer, sprinkle with grated cheddar cheese and crumbled bacon bits. Serve with sour cream and chives.

BAKE-FRIED POTATO CAKES

Use left-over baked potatoes, 3–5 potatoes. Scrape out potato filling and mash with fork or potato masher. Add 1 c. sour cream, ½ c. cheddar cheese, 2 tbsp. buttermilk, 1 c. flour. Mix together and spoon into hot greased skilled. Fry until golden brown; flip; and fry until done. Serve with ketchup.

KENTUCKY COLONELS

½ stick butter
1 box (1 lb.) chopped dates
1 cup sugar

Mix above ingredients and cook over medium heat for 4-5 minutes. Stand off heat. Add ½ cup chopped nuts and 2-½ cups Rice Krispies. After cooled, roll into balls and roll in coconut.

COTTAGE CHEESE SALAD

1 carton cottage cheese
1 tbsp. sugar
1 onion chopped
1 green pepper chopped
½ c. mayo
1 tomato chopped

Stir in all ingredients together and chill for 12 hours.

SIMPLE BEAN SOUP

1 pound package white Northern beans
2 c. chopped smoked ham
Salt & Pepper
4 c. chopped carrots
4 c. chopped celery

Cover with water and simmer slowly for 4 to 5 hours. Occasionally stirring and checking water level.

BANANA BREAD

Mash 3 ripe bananas
2 c. flour
1 tsp. salt
1 tsp. soda

½ c. wheat germ
½ c. melted butter
2 eggs
1 c. apple juice

Mix dry ingredients together, add remaining ingredients. Bake in greased loaf pan for 1 hour at 350 degrees.

FROSTED GINGER PEOPLE

⅓ c. margarine
⅓ c. sugar
⅓ c. dark molasses
1 egg
1 tsp. ginger

½ tsp. soda
Dash of salt
3 c. sifted confectioners sugar
¼ c. milk
½ tsp. vanilla

Cream margarine and sugar until light and fluffy. Blend in molasses and egg. Add combined dry ingredients; mix well. Chill, roll out dough on lightly floured surface to ⅛-inch thickness; cut with gingerbread cutters. Place on greased cookie sheets, bake at 375 degrees for 8 to 10 minutes or until edges are very lightly browned. Cool.

Combine sugar, milk, vanilla, and salt; mix well. Frost cookies. Decorate with raisins and candies, if desired. Makes about 3-½ dozen 3-inch cookies.

QUICK DINNER ROLLS

1 c. warm water
1 pkg. dry yeast
2 tbsp. sugar
1-¼ c. sifted flour (Gold Medal)

1 tsp. salt
1 egg
2 tbsp. soft shortening

Dissolve yeast in mixing bowl with warm water. Stir in sugar, flour, egg, shortening and salt. Beat until smooth. Scrape down sides of bowl and cover with a cloth. Let rise in a warm place for 45 minutes. Work down dough and make into dinner rolls, and let rise again. Bake at 400 degrees until golden brown.

CONFETTI MALLOW POPCORN BALLS

4 c. miniature marshmallows
½ c. margarine
½ tsp. vanilla

¼ tsp. salt
3 qts. Unsalted popped corn
1-½ c. chopped gumdrops

Melt marshmallows with margarine in saucepan over low heat; stir occasionally until smooth. Stir in vanilla and salt. Pour mixture over combined popped corn and gumdrops; toss lightly until well coated. With hands slightly moistened with water, shape 1-½ inch balls; place on greased baking sheet. Makes 3 dozen balls.

FUDGY PIE

Mix together 1-½ c. flour, 2 c. sugar, and 5 tbsp. cocoa. Add 2 sticks of melted butter. Stir in eggs and vanilla. Pour into 9" pie pan. Bake at 350° about 30 minutes. Cool before cutting. (30 minutes: center is pudding, outer is chewy; 45 minutes: center chewy, outer edge dried)

CHOCOLATE SHEET CAKE

1-¼ c. margarine or butter	1 c. nuts
1 c. water	½ c. unsweetened cocoa
2 c. unsifted flour	1 tsp. ground cinnamon
1 tsp. soda	
1-½ c. firmly packed brown sugar	
1 (14 oz.) can Eagle Brand Sweetened Condensed Milk	
½ tsp. salt.	2 eggs
1 tsp. vanilla	1 c. confectioner's sugar

Preheat oven to 350 degrees. In small saucepan, melt 1 c. margarine; stir in ¼ c. cocoa then water. Bring to boil; remove from heat. In large mixing bowl, combine flour, brown sugar, soda, cinnamon, and salt. Add cocoa mixture, beat well. Stir ⅓ c. Eagle Brand, eggs, and vanilla. Pour into greased 15" x 10" jelly roll pan. Bake 15 minutes or until cake springs back when lightly touched. In small saucepan, melt remaining ¼ c. margarine; stir in remaining ¼ c. cocoa and Eagle Brand. Stir in confectioners sugar and nuts. Spread on warm cake.

JAN'S SWEET AND SOUR CABBAGE

1 tbsp. bacon grease	3 tbsp. brown sugar
1 big spoon pickle relish	1 c. water
1 head cabbage chopped & chilled	
Seasonings: salt and pepper to taste	

Boil down on high until tender.

TAB'S BAKED BEANS

Soak 1 lb. of navy beans overnight. Cook in 1-½ quarts water, 2 slices bacon, salt and pepper to taste about 40 minutes, on medium high heat until almost dry. Pour beans and liquid into casserole dish. Add 2 chopped onions, 1 c. ketchup or tomato sauce, 1 c. molasses. Top with 3 strips of bacon. Bake at 350 degrees for 1 hour.

KUSHAW

Cut kushaw into 2" x 4" squares, place meat side down in electric skillet with ½ cup water, ½ stick butter, ground allspice, cinnamon, and nutmeg to taste, add ½ c. brown sugar and additional ½ cup water. Simmer covered for 1 hour, or until meat is tender.

YELLOW SQUASH

3 small to medium sized yellow (summer) squash, sliced thin
½ stick butter   ¼ c. brown sugar
½ c. water   1 tsp. ground allspice

Simmer squash in skillet with all ingredients until tender. Serve.

MACARONI AND TOMATOES

2 c. macaroni, cooked and drained
1 can tomatoes
1 tsp. garlic salt   ½ stick butter
2 tbsp. flour   ½ c. sugar

Melt butter, stir in flour, add cooked macaroni, add tomatoes, sugar and garlic salt. Simmer until thickened.

ELSIE'S SOUR CREAM POUND CAKE

2 sticks real butter (no substitute)
3 cups plain flour   6 eggs
2-2/3 cup sugar
1/2 tsp. soda   1 tsp. vanilla
1 (8 oz.) carton sour cream

Cream butter and sugar well. Add eggs one at a time and mix well. Stir in sour cream with soda in it, mix in flour to mixture, add vanilla last and bake in tube pan in a 325 degree oven for 1 hour or a little longer. I test my cakes with toothpicks, don't open the door on cake. Cool before removing cake from pan.

I make a glaze out of powdered sugar and lemon juice. Just mix and pour over cake, put in oven under broiler and when the glaze starts to bubble, take out, must watch this closely.

MAMAW'S RICE PUDDING

2 eggs   2 tsp. vanilla
1/2 c. sugar   2 c. cooked rice
1/2 tsp. salt   Dash of nutmeg
2-1/4 c. milk

Separate eggs, Beat yolks, add sugar, salt, milk, vanilla, and rice. Stiffly beat egg whites and fold into mixture, turn into baking dish. Sprinkle with nutmeg. Bake at 350 degrees for 45 minutes. Serves 6.

ELSIE'S RHUBARB SALAD

1 cup sugar
2 cups cooked rhubarb
6 oz. package strawberry jello
8 oz. cream cheese
1 cup boiling water

16 oz. can crushed pineapple
1 cup chopped apples

12 oz. cool whip

Mix sugar with rhubarb, mix jello with boiling water. Add to rhubarb mixture, add pineapple and apples. Mix well and pour into 11" x 13" pan. Chill until set, blend cream cheese and cool whip, spread on top of jello, sprinkle with nuts.

ELSIE'S HOT ROLLS

2 cups water (let come to boil)
Mix:
½ cup sugar
¾ cup shortening
1 tsp. salt

Set off and let cool.

Dissolve 2 packages yeast in 2 tbsp. warm water.
2 beaten eggs
When above is cool, mix all together and add 3 cups flour.
Mix well.
Then add about 4 more cups flour until it pulls away from the side of the pan.
Grease a large bowl with lid.
Put dough in bowl and put a little melted butter over the top.
Punch down when needed.
Refrigerate over night, roll out the next day about ¼ inch, cutout with biscuit cutter. Dip in melted butter, fold over, and put in a warm place until double in size. Bake in 400 degree oven until brown.

ELSIE'S APPLE CINNAMON ROLLS

1 stick butter
2 cups sugar
2 cups water
1-½ cups self-rising flour

½ cup shortening
⅓ cup milk
2 cups chopped apples
1 tsp. cinnamon

This looks like too much liquid but the crust will absorb it. Heat oven to 350 degrees, melt butter in a 13" x 9" x 2" pan. In saucepan heat sugar and water until sugar melts real good and hot. Mix flour and shortening like pie crust and add milk, roll dough into a large rectangle about ¼ inch thick, sprinkle apples over the dough and roll like a jelly roll, slice into about 16 slices ½ inch thick and place in pan of butter. Pour sugar syrup carefully around rolls, sprinkle cinnamon over top and bake in 350 degree oven for 55 to 60 minutes.

UNCLE JIM'S
BLACK RASPBERRY COBBLER – DUMPLINGS

Mix together:
2 cups black raspberries
1 cup water
½ cup sugar

Bring to boil and add dumplings
¾ cup self-rising flour
1 tbsp. Crisco
¼ cup buttermilk

Roll dough on cutting board, cut dumplings and drop in hot berry mixture. Cook 8 to 10 minutes. Line baking dish with your favorite pie crust. Pour in berry-dumpling mixture, dot with butter, top with pie crust. Bake 400 degrees until brown, 25 to 30 minutes.

AUNT LORETTA'S CORN PUDDING

1 can whole kernel corn
1 can cream style corn

Mix together:
4 tbsp. flour
1 tsp. salt.

Combine with above:
2 cups milk
2 eggs, well beaten
1 tbsp. butter

Mix well. Pour into well-greased baking dish. Bake 1 hour in 350 degree oven. Stir 3 times first 30 minutes (away from sides and bottom). You can use fresh, or home frozen, or home canned corn. Increase baking time about 30 minutes for fresh corn.

SHUCKIE BEANS

To make shuck beans you dry fresh green beans that are strung and snapped. (White half runners are a good bean to dry.) Place broken beans on a newspaper in a dry dark place (such as an attic). Give them about 6 to 8 weeks, checking and turning occasionally.

Measure about 2 lbs. of beans and place in large container. Cover beans with water, add 1 tsp. salt. Soak overnight.
Next day: Drain water from beans and cover with fresh water.

Add:
1 tsp. salt
Pepper to taste

1 tbsp. bacon drippings
1 slab fresh salt pork

Cook beans down on high heat for about 20 minutes. Reduce heat and simmer about 2 hours checking water level so that they don't cook too dry.

KILT LETTUCE

Wash and dry about 25 pieces of leaf lettuce. Place lettuce in large bowl and add 2–3 chopped green onions.

Heat 8 tablespoons bacon drippings and pour over lettuce and onion. Serve immediately.

CORN RELISH

12 ears corn   12 green peppers
12 cucumbers   10 onions
4 hot peppers

Cut up above ingredients
4 c. sugar   4 c. white vinegar
5 tbsp. mustard   5 tbsp. salt
1 tsp. turmeric

Mix above ingredients and pour over vegetables. Cook for 25 minutes and place in clean jars and seal.

SQUASH PICKLES

8 c. small squash, sliced   2 c. green peppers, sliced
2 c. onion, sliced
2 c. red peppers, or 4 oz. jar pimento

Salt vegetables to taste and let stand in water for 1 hour. (Use pickling salt.)

Combine:
2 c. white vinegar   2 tsp. celery seeds
2-½ c. sugar   2 tsp. whole mustard seeds

Drain vegetables. Bring vinegar mixture to a boil and add vegetables. Continue to boil. In bottom of clean hot jars, place ⅛ tsp. alum. Pour pickles in jars and seal.

MACARONI SALAD

2 c. macaroni, elbow style
Boiled in 1 quart water and 1 tbsp. cooking oil. Drain and cool.

2 stalks celery, chopped	1 green pepper, chopped
1 red pepper, chopped	1 c. mayo
1 small onion, chopped	3 tbsp. celery seed
1 small jar pimento, chopped	2 tbsp. yellow prepared mustard
4 eggs boiled and chopped	3 tbsp. pickle relish

Stir well and chill for 1 hour.

POTATO SALAD

6 medium potatoes, peeled, chopped, and cooked al dente
1 c. mayo   2 tbsp. yellow prepared mustard
Stir into warm potatoes.
Add:

½ c. chopped celery	½ c. chopped green pepper
½ c. onion, chopped	3 tbsp. pickle relish
4 eggs, boiled and chopped	3 tbsp. celery seed

1 jar (small) pimento, chopped and drained
Mix well and chill for 1 hour.

DEVILED EGGS

6 eggs, Grade A large, boiled hard. **Always boil refrigerated eggs in cold water to start process. Turn eggs every 2 minutes with spoon. Peel eggs and halve. Separate yellows and place in small bowl, mash with fork.

Add:

2 tsp. pickle relish	1 tbsp. mayo
1 tsp. vinegar	½ tsp. celery seed
1 tsp. sugar	Salt and pepper to taste
1 tbsp. yellow prepared mustard	

Stir well and fill egg whites with yolk mixture. Garnish with paprika. Chill.

SIN PIE

Set out:
1 quart ice cream (any flavor)
2 packages of Ritz snack crackers (approx. 45 crackers)
1 stick butter melted

Crush crackers fine, drizzle melted butter over crackers and press down into a 9" x 13" pan.

2 small boxes or 1 large box of instant pudding (any flavor)
Fix pudding as directed on box and blend with a wire whisk. Blend in ice cream with pudding and pour over crackers then freeze (about 2 hours).

Before serving, remove from freezer and top with Cool Whip. Sprinkle with nut topping and brickle.

Choose a flavor of ice cream you can match with pudding flavor.

RICE PUDDING

6 eggs
1 c. milk
1 c. sugar
2 c. uncooked rice

1 tsp. vanilla
1 tsp. cinnamon
1 c. raisins (optional)

Stir together and back at 350 degrees for 30 minutes. Check every 10 minutes for dryness, if needed add more milk.

POTATO SOUP

10 potatoes, peeled and diced
3 c. water
BOIL.

Add:
1 c. chopped celery
1 c. chopped onion
2 bay leaves

1 can carnation cream
1 stick butter
½ c. milk

When potatoes are done, add remaining ingredients and simmer until done.

GOLDEN RAISIN CARROT CAKE

1-¼ c. unsifted flour
1 tsp. baking powder
½ tsp. baking soda
½ tsp. salt
½ tsp. cinnamon
4 eggs, separated

½ c. firmly packed brown sugar
½ c. peanut oil
¼ c. water
1 c. coarsely grated raw carrots
½ c. white seedless raisins
2 tbsp. grated lemon peel

Combine flour, baking soda, baking powder, salt, and cinnamon, and set aside.

Beat egg whites in small mixing bowl until soft peaks form, set aside.

In a large bowl combine sugar and peanut oil. Beat until well blended. Combine egg yolks and water. Stir into egg mixture. Mix in carrots, raisins, and lemon peel. Blend in dry ingredients. Fold in egg whites. Turn batter into well-greased bundt pan or a ring mold pan.

Bake at 350 degrees for 50 minutes or until done. Cool on wire rack for 10 minutes in pan, then out of pan for another 45 minutes.

MARIETTA'S MUDD AND SNOW CAKE

Prepare Devils Food Cake per directions.
Fill ⅔ full in an oblong pan.

Mix together:
8 oz. cream cheese   ⅓ c. sugar
1 egg
Stir in 6 oz. mini chocolate chips

Drop into cake by tablespoonfuls
Bake 350 degrees for 25 minutes.

Both of these recipes were given to me by my Dad, Leonard McCoy, the best hillbilly chef in the state of Kentucky.

APPLE PIE

3 c. chopped apples	1 tsp. cloves
1 tsp. allspice	1 tsp. cinnamon
1 tsp. nutmeg	1 tsp. vanilla
1 egg yolk	1 stick butter
1 c. sugar	1 oz. Amaretto

Mix all ingredients together and pour into homemade pie crust or Pillsbury All-Ready crust and bake at 350 degrees for 1 hour; reduce heat to 300 degrees the last 10 minutes.

STRAWBERRY SHORTCAKE

3 c. fresh strawberries, sliced in halves
2 c. sugar
Stir together and refrigerate

Yellow Cake:

2-½ c. flour	2 eggs
¾ c. sugar	1 tsp. vanilla
½ c. milk	

Stir together and pour into 9" x 13" aluminum cake pan. Bake at 350 degrees for 30 minutes. Cool cake and split. Cut into squares. Layer cake and strawberries; top with whipped cream (Daddy's favorite).

PEACH PIE

Crust:

2 c. flour
¾ c. ice water

1 c. shortening, or 1 stick
    softened butter

Cut shortening into flour, add ice water, a little at a time. Roll out on floured counter top. Place in pie pan. Reserve enough crust for topping.

Filling:

3 c. diced peaches, fresh
1 tsp. cinnamon
1 tsp. cloves

1 c. sugar
1 tsp. allspice
1 stick butter, cut into pats

Mix together and pour into pie crust. Put reserve crust on top of pie filling and pinch crust. Take a fork around the edges and flute edges. With a sharp buttered knife, cut 3 diamond shapes into center of pie. Bake at 375 degrees for 45 minutes.

QUICK CHICKEN AND DUMPLINGS

5 Chicken breasts, split
2 (10-½ oz.) cans cream of chicken soup
1 package frozen peas and carrots
¾ c. milk   2 c. Bisquick mix
¼ tsp. sage   2 tbsp shortening
2 tsp. parsley

Using 12" skillet, brown chicken lightly in shortening. Then add soup, simmer for 1 hour. Add vegetables. In another bowl mix Bisquick, milk, sage, and parsley. Drop by spoonfuls around chicken. Cover and simmer 15-20 minutes.

FRIED APPLES

4 to 6 Yellow Delicious Apples, peeled and sliced
2 tbsp. bacon grease
1 c. water
1 c. sugar

In sauce pot, add all ingredients and stir once. Boil down hard on high heat until almost dry. Juice should resemble syrup texture. Serve hot with biscuits, gravy and fried eggs.

MOTHER'S APPLESAUCE RAISIN BREAD

1-½ c. flour
1 tsp. baking powder
1 tsp. cinnamon
1 c. quick oats
2 eggs
1 c. applesauce

1 tsp. baking soda
1 tsp. salt
½ tsp. nutmeg
½ c. firmly packed brown sugar
⅓ c. salad oil
1 c. raisins

Combine dry ingredients, add eggs, oil, and applesauce. Stir until combined. Stir in raisins. Fill loaf pan and bake at 350 degrees for 1 hour. Loaf pan should be greased and floured.

BUTTERMILK PIE WITH A HINT OF LEMON

3 eggs
1-¾ c. sugar
1 tbsp. corn meal
½ c. buttermilk
3 tbsp. flour

1 stick butter, melted
1 tsp. vanilla
1 tsp. lemon juice
1 tbsp. lemon rind
3 or 4 tbsp. coconut (optional)

Preheat oven to 425°. Mix all ingredients together and pour into Pillsbury unbaked pie shell. Bake for 10 minutes at 425°, then lower temperature to 325° and continue baking for 35 minutes.

APPLE STREUSEL MINCE PIE

1 (9-inch) unbaked pastry shell
3 all-purpose apples, pared and thinly sliced
3 tbsp. unsifted flour
2 tbsp. margarine, melted
1 (28 oz.) jar None Such Ready to Use Mincemeat
Streusel topping

Preheat oven to 425 degrees. In large bow, toss apples with flour and margarine, arrange in pastry shell. Top with mincemeat, then streusel topping. Bake 10 minutes. Reduce heat to 375 degrees, continue baking 25 minutes or until golden brown. Cool slightly. Serve warm.

Streusel Topping:
In bowl, combine ½ cup unsifted flour, ¼ cup firmly packed brown sugar and 1 teaspoon ground cinnamon, cut in ⅓ cup cold margarine until crumbly. Add ¼ cup chopped nuts.

NO BAKE PUMPKIN PIE

1 egg
1 (14 oz.) can Eagle Brand sweetened condensed milk
1 tsp. ground cinnamon
½ tsp. each ground ginger, nutmeg, and salt
1 envelope Knox unflavored gelatin
2 tbsp. water
1 (16 oz.) can pumpkin
1 Keebler Ready Crust graham cracker crust

In medium bowl, beat egg, beat in Eagle Brand, and spices. In a medium saucepan, sprinkle gelatin over water, let stand 1 minute. Over low heat stir until gelatin dissolves. Add Eagle Brand mixture, over low heat, cook and stir until mixture thickens slightly, 5 to 10 minutes. Remove from heat, stir in pumpkin. Pour into crust. Chill 4 hours or until set.

GRANNY'S CHICKEN AND DUMPLINGS

Cook and strain chicken. Debone.
Dough: Judge to amount by measuring 5 cups plain flour and 3 eggs

Mix flour and eggs together and roll out and cut. Have broth ready to boil and add ¼ teaspoon yellow food coloring. Drop dough into boiling broth and cook until done. Do not stir. Pour ½ can evaporated milk into dumplings. Stir once after adding milk.

BROWN BAG FRIED CHICKEN

Take 1 grocery brown bag. Make sure bag is clean and empty. Put 2 cups flour, 1 tbsp. seasoned salt and 1 tbsp. seasoned pepper, 1 tsp. poultry seasoning, 1 tsp. meat tenderizer, ¼ tsp. garlic powder, ½ tsp. Mrs. Dash. Roll top of brown bag down about ¼ of the way. Shake well. Wash chicken and dry on paper towels. Salt and pepper chicken. Dip into 1 cup buttermilk and 1 beaten egg. Throw the chicken in the brown bag and shake well. Remove chicken from bag, and fry in hot cooking oil in electric or cast iron skillet until golden brown. Turning occasionally.

BANANA NUT BREAD

1-½ c. all purpose flour
¾ tsp. baking soda
½ tsp. salt
1 c. sugar
2 eggs slightly beaten

3 tbsp. buttermilk
⅔ mashed bananas (1 cup)
½ c. chopped pecans
¾ c. oil

Preheat oven to 325 degrees. Grease and flour loaf pan. Sift flour, baking soda, and salt. Add sugar, eggs, oil, and buttermilk. Stir well, fold in bananas, add nuts. Pour into loaf pan and bake for 1 hour or until toothpick comes out clean. Cool in pan 15 to 30 minutes, turn on wire rack.

PEANUT BUTTER COOKIES

3 c. flour
1 c. sugar
1 tsp. baking soda
1 stick margarine

1 c. peanut butter
2 eggs
1 tsp. vanilla

Add all ingredients together and drop by teaspoonfuls onto baking sheet and bake for 8 minutes.

CORNBREAD

2 c. cornmeal mix (Martha White)
1-½ c. flour, self-rising
1 egg
1 tsp. sugar

1 c. buttermilk
Dash salt
2 tbsp. cooking oil

Mix all together and pour into greased skillet and bake at 425 degrees for 25 minutes or until golden brown.

BISCUITS

3 c. self-rising flour
1 c. buttermilk

⅓ c. Crisco shortening

Mix together and roll out onto floured counter or wax paper. Cut into biscuits, topped with a little butter or margarine. Bake at 400 degrees for 15 minutes or slightly brown.

PONE BREAD

3 c. self-rising flour
¼ c. warm water

1 c. buttermilk

Stir together. Pour into greased skillet. Bake at 400 degrees for 15-20 minutes.

CREAM STYLE CORNBREAD

2 c. corn meal mix
1 can cream style corn
1 tbsp. cooking oil
Dash sugar

1 c. flour
1 egg
Salt

Mix well and pour into greased skillet. Bake at 425 degrees for 20 minutes.

MAW'S FRIED CORNBREAD

1 c. corn meal mix
½ c. buttermilk

½ c. flour
4 tbsp. warm water

Stir together and pour into hot greased skillet and fry until golden brown on each side.

ALMA'S PRUNE CAKE

1-½ c. sugar
1 c. milk soured (buttermilk)
1 c. Wesson oil
2 c. flour
3 eggs
1 c. pecans or walnuts

1 tsp. baking soda
1 tsp. vanilla
1 tsp. cinnamon
1 tsp. allspice
1 c. chopped prunes (cooked)

Mix all ingredients, beat 2 minutes. Fold in 1 cup of cooked chopped prunes. Fold 1 cup chopped pecans or walnuts. Bake 300 degrees for 1 hour.

PRUNE CAKE SAUCE

1 c. sugar   ½ c. buttermilk
1 stick butter   1 tsp. baking soda

Boil for 5 minutes. Pour over warm cake.

JAM CAKE

3-½ c. flour (use Cake flour)   2 c. sugar
1 tsp. baking soda   1 c. margarine
1 tsp. cloves   1 c. sour milk (buttermilk)
1 tsp. cinnamon   4 eggs
1 tsp. allspice   1 c. jam (blackberry with seeds)
1 tsp. vanilla

Mix together all ingredients in large bowl until smooth. Pour into well-greased bundt pan and bake at 350 degrees for 45 minutes to 1 hour. To check for proper doneness press with fingertips the center of cake; it will spring back lightly. Turn upside-down to cool.

For a holiday appearance cover the cake with a lace doily and sprinkle with confectioners sugar. Remove doily and you have a snowflake effect.

RUBY MCCOY'S COCA-COLA CAKE

2 c. unsifted flour
2 c. sugar
1 tsp. baking soda
3 tbsp. cocoa
1 c. Coca-Cola

½ c. buttermilk
2 beaten eggs
2 sticks Blue Bonnet margarine
1 tsp. vanilla
1-½ c. miniature marshmallows

Combine flour and sugar. Heat butter, cocoa, and Coca-Cola until it boils. Pour over flour mixture. MIX WELL. Add buttermilk, eggs, baking soda, vanilla, and marshmallows. Beat well. Pour into a well-greased pan 9" x 13" flat. Bake at 350 degrees for 40 minutes and check. Baking time may vary according to ovens and altitude. Sometimes it takes 50 minutes.

COCA-COLA ICING

1 c. chopped pecans
3 tbsp. cocoa
1 box confectioner's sugar

½ c. butter
6 tbsp. Coca-Cola

Combine butter, cocoa, and Coca-Cola. Bring to a boil. Pour over sugar and beat well. Add nuts, spread over hot cake.

SADIE MCCOY'S QUICK DINNER ROLLS

1 pkg. yeast
¼ c. sugar
¼ c. soft shortening
2-½ c. bread flour or regular flour

1 c. warm water
1 tsp. salt
2 eggs

In large bowl, add warm water, yeast, sugar and salt; let sit for 3 to 5 minutes. Add about half of the flour and mix well; add shortening and eggs and the rest of the flour; mixing well. Put on floured pastry cloth or counter top and knead until elastic feeling. Let rise until double bulk; knead again until all bubbles are gone. Make into desirable rolls and bake at 400 degrees for 15 to 20 minutes.

PECAN TASTIES

Shells:
1 package (3 oz.) cream cheese softened
1 stick butter, softened
1 c. all-purpose flour

Combine cream cheese and butter; cream until smooth. Add flour, mix well. Refrigerate dough 1 hour, then shape into 24-1" balls. Place balls in mini-muffin pans. Press dough against bottom and sides. Shaping into shells.

Filling:
¾ c. dark brown sugar, firmly packed
½ tsp. vanilla
1 egg slightly beaten   ¼ tsp. salt
1 tbsp. butter, melted   ½ c. pecans, chopped

Combine brown sugar, egg, butter, salt, and vanilla, mix well. Spoon into pastry shells, and bake at 350 degrees for 25 minutes. Top with ½ pecan pieces if desired.

BREAD & BUTTER PICKLES

Slice and place in ice water for 3 hours:
½ c. salt   ½ peck cucumbers
6 onions   6 peppers

Mix:
1 c. sugar   2 c. apple cider vinegar
3 tsp. pickling spices   3 tsp. mustard seed
3 tsp. celery seed

Mix these ingredients together and bring to a boil, add the drained cucumbers, peppers, and onions. Taste to tell. Place in clean jars and seal.

PIE EATING CAKE

1 box Duncan Hines Yellow Cake Mix
4 eggs
½ c. oil   1 c. mandarin oranges

Mix cake mix with above ingredients and bake according to package directions.

1 (8 oz.) container whipped topping
1 c. crushed pineapple, drained
1 box instant vanilla pudding

Mix the above 3 ingredients and ice cake. Decorate cake with cherries and sprinkle cake with coconut.

KUSHAW PIE

Yield: 2 pies

4 c. cooked kushaw   4 eggs
1 c. brown sugar   1 c. white sugar
2 tbsp. pumpkin pie spice   1 can condensed milk

Mix all ingredients and pour into two pie shells. Bake at 350° for 40–50 minutes. Check pie with toothpick in center after 40 minutes.

– 2 –

APPETIZERS & BEVERAGES

NOTES

CHRISTMAS CHEESE BALL

1 (8 oz.) package Philly cream cheese
1 (8 oz.) tub Old Port Wine cheese
½ c. shredded cheddar cheese
1 c. chopped pecans
1 dash red food coloring

Mix all ingredients except nuts well with hands until smooth. Roll in the chopped nuts until fully covered. Chill.

PINEAPPLE CHEESE BALL

1 (8 oz.) package Philly cream cheese
1 jar pineapple neufatchel cheese
1 c. chopped pecans

Mix cheese and roll in nuts. Chill.

SWEDISH MEATBALLS

1 lb. ground round
1 pkg. onion soup mix

2 tsp. Worcestershire sauce
⅔ c. milk

Mix well and roll into balls. Broil on 400 degrees about 10 minutes or until brown. Place in crock pot.

Sauce:
2 c. ketchup
¼ c. brown sugar

2 tbsp. Worcestershire sauce

Mix well. In separate pan simmer this mixture for 10 minutes. Pour over meatballs and simmer for 1 hour.

"PHILLY" CHEESE BELL

8 oz. pkg. Cracker Barrel brand sharp cheddar cheese
2 tsp. chopped pimento   2 tsp. chopped green pepper
2 tsp. chopped onion   1 tsp Worcestershire sauce
8 oz. pkg. Philadelphia cream cheese
2 tbsp. margarine   ½ tsp. lemon juice

Combine cold pack cheese food, cream cheese, and 2 table-spoons margarine; mix until well blended. Add remaining ingre-dients; mix well. Mold into 2 cold pack containers coated with margarine or lined plastic wrap. Chill until firm; unmold. Garnish with chopped parsley and pimento strips, if desired. 2 bells.

MINIATURE SAUSAGE PIZZA

1 lb. sausage, hot, Italian, or mild
1 tsp. cumin   ½ tsp. garlic powder
16 oz. can pizza sauce   6 oz. tomato paste
Oregano   6 sourdough muffins
1 c. shredded mozzarella cheese
Fennel

Brown sausage, garlic powder, and cumin in preheated skillet, drain. Mix tomato paste and can pizza sauce, spread 2 tbsp. mixture on each half of muffins. Top with sausage, oregano, and fennel to taste, and mozzarella. Bake 5 minutes at 400 degrees or 1 minute at 400 degrees in microwave. Makes 12 mini pizzas.

POPEYE'S SPINACH DIP

½ c. parsley
1 pkg. frozen chopped spinach, cooked and drained
2 c. mayo   2 small green onions, chopped

Mix all ingredients together. Chill. Serve with fresh vegetables.

SAUSAGE CHEESE BALLS

1 lb. hot sausage
8 oz. sharp cheddar cheese, grated
3 c. Bisquick

Mix ingredients with a fork. Shape into 1-inch balls. Place on ungreased cookie sheet and bake at 325 degrees from 12 to 15 minutes or until done. These appetizers may be frozen. Thaw slightly before baking and increase cooking time. Makes about 40 to 50 balls.

PARTY SLOPPY JOES

½ lb. ground beef
¼ c. chopped onion
½ lb. frankfurters
¾ c. barbeque sauce

¼ c. sweet pickle relish
Hamburger buns, split
Velveeta cheese

Brown meat, drain. Add onion and cook until tender. Add frankfurters, barbeque sauce and pickle relish. Cover, simmer for 15 minutes. For each sandwich, cover bottom half of bun with Velveeta cheese slice, top with meet mixture. Serve with top half of bun. 8 sandwiches.

PETITES QUICHES

Pastry for unbaked pie crust (9 inch)
Dash of pepper   ¾ c. half and half
4 oz. Swiss cheese, sliced, and chopped
2 eggs, slightly beaten   1 tbsp. flour
¼ tsp. salt
4 strips bacon cooked and crumbled

Line miniature muffin pans with pastry. Combine half and half, eggs, and seasonings; mix well. Toss cheese with flour, add cheese and bacon to egg mixture. Fill muffin shells, two-thirds full with egg and cheese mixture. Bake at 325 degrees for 30 to 35 minutes or until lightly browned. Makes 24 appetizers.

ARTICHOKE DIP

1 can artichoke hearts, cut up in small pieces
1 c. Parmesan cheese   1 c. grated Swiss cheese
1 c. mayo

Mix all ingredients together and bake at 350 degrees for 30 minutes. Serve with Wheat Thin crackers.

FRUIT-N-CHEESE APPETIZER

8 oz. pkg. Philadelphia cream cheese
½ c. shredded cheddar cheese
½ c. salad dressing   ½ c. finely chopped apple

Combine softened cream cheese, and salad dressing; mixing until well blended. Add cheese and apple; mix well. Chill. Serve with apple wedges, crackers, and party rye bread. 1-⅔ cups.

HOLIDAY VEGETABLE DIP

8 oz. bottle Thousand Island dressing
2 tbsp. green onion slices   Assorted fresh vegetables
1 hard cooked egg, chopped

Combine dressing, egg, and green onion; mix lightly. Chill. Serve with vegetable dippers. Makes about 1 cup.

CARAMEL ORANGE FONDUE

14 oz. bag Kraft caramels   Pound cake cubes
½ c. pure orange juice   ¼ tsp. grated orange rind
Toasted slivered almonds

Melt caramels with orange juice in covered double broiler or in saucepan over low heat. Stir occasionally until sauce is smooth; add orange rind. Pour into fondue pot. Keep warm while serving. Dip cake into caramel sauce, roll into nuts. 1-⅓ cups.

DIP FOR FRIED VEGETABLES

½ c. mayo   ¼ c. horseradish
Dash salt and pepper   ¼ tsp lemon juice

Stir ingredients together until creamy.

CHUNKY CHICKEN SANDWICHES

1 lb. boned and skinned chicken breasts
¼ tsp. pepper   1 scallion
8 slices crusty bread   ¾ c. mayo
8 thin slices prosciutto ham   1 tsp. whole grain mustard
1 c. watercress leaves

Put the chicken breasts in a saucepan with ¼ cup water. Bring
to a simmer, cover and cook until springy to the touch, 6 to 8
minutes. To cook in a microwave oven, put the chicken and
¼ cup water in microwave proof baking dish. Cover with plastic
wrap and poke holes in plastic. Microwave on high 4 minutes
and let stand 5 minutes longer. Drain chicken cooked by either
method and let cool. Cut chicken into ½ " cubes. Chop scallion.
Mix chicken with scallion, mayo, mustard, salt and pepper. Top
4 slices of bread with the ham, chicken, watercress, and another
slice of bread.

CHEESE SAUCE

½ stick butter   ½ c. half and half
8 oz. chopped block cheese (Velveeta, cheddar, or Swiss)

In small sauce pot, slowly melt cheese with half and half and
butter. Serve warm.

**Great used for: dipping fried or raw vegetables, over fresh
steamed broccoli, baked potatoes, and steamed cauliflower.

AVOCADO DIP

1 large ripe avocado, peeled and chopped
1 small onion, minced   1 tsp. seasoned salt
4 tbsp. mayo   Garlic salt
1 tsp. seasoned pepper

Puree all ingredients in blender, add 1 tsp of lemon juice (keep avocado green). Serve with tortilla chips, fresh vegetables, on taco salads as garnish.

FRENCH ONION DIP

1 small container sour cream
1 envelope Lipton's onion soup mix
Dash lemon juice   Dash Worcestershire sauce
1 tbsp. mayo

Stir together and serve chilled.

MIMI'S PINK PUNCH

1 qt. apple juice, chilled
1 pt. cranberry cocktail juice, chilled
1 bottle of ginger ale, chilled
¼ c. lemon juice   2 c. ice cubes
Raspberry sherbet

In punch bowl, combine juices and ice. Add ginger ale, top with scoops of sherbet.

ELSIE'S RED CHRISTMAS PUNCH

1 small pkg. red jello   1 c. boiling water
1 (6 oz.) can frozen orange juice
1 (6 oz.) can frozen pineapple juice
3 c. cold water   1 qt. cranberry juice
1 qt. ginger ale

Mix jello in boiling water. Stir in juices. Add cold water and
cranberry juice. Just before serving, add 1 quart ginger ale.

ELAINE'S LIME SHERBET PUNCH

1 liter 7-Up   1 liter ginger ale
1 half gallon lime sherbet

In punch bowl, put in lime sherbet. Pour equal amounts of 7-Up
and ginger ale over top of sherbet. Let sherbet melt. Stirring
occasionally.

HAM & CHEESE ROLLS

1 jar candied dill strip pickles, drained
1 pkg. boiled ham, sliced
1 pkg. Velveeta cheese slices

Places ham flat down, turn side ways, lay cheese on top of ham;
place pickle in center and fold over "baby diaper" style. Place
toothpick in center to hold in place. Serve as Hors D'oeuvres.

PIGS IN A BLANKET

1 pkg. cocktail style wieners
1 lb. sliced cheese, any variety
2 cans country style biscuits

On floured counter top, roll out biscuits thin and flat. Place one slice cheese and one wiener in center, roll up. Bake as directed on biscuit can. Serve as an appetizer.

SAUSAGE BALLS

1 lb. pkg. mild sausage
1 (16 oz.) pkg. shredded cheddar cheese
2 c. Bisquick

Mix all ingredients together well. Form into balls and bake at 400 degrees for 15 minutes.

COCKTAIL WIENER SKEWERS

1 small jar hot cocktail wieners, drained
1 dozen cheese cubes, any variety
1 small jar Spanish olives, drained

On a toothpick or cocktail skewer, stack one wiener, one cube of cheese, and one olive.

*This makes a great party tray. Roll a grapefruit in foil; spear wiener skewers all around the grapefruit except for the bottom.

BAKED STUFFED MUSHROOMS

1 (8 oz.) pkg. cream cheese, softened to room temperature
1 lb. pkg. fresh mushrooms, washed and stemmed
10 strips of bacon, cooked crisp and crumbled
1 c. grated cheddar cheese

Mix together softened cream cheese and bacon. Stuff mushrooms with cream cheese mixture. Place stuffing side up in a greased casserole dish, cover with grated cheddar cheese. Bake at 350 degrees for 15 to 20 minutes or until cheese is melted.

WALNUT-BRIE TORTA

3 oz. cream cheese, at room temperature
2 tbsp. light cream
1-½ c. coarsely chopped walnuts
1 wheel (8 oz.) Brie of Camembert chest, chilled
Grape clusters

In a mixing bowl, beat the cream cheese with a fork or wooden spoon until smooth. Gradually stir in walnuts until well blended. With a sharp knife split cheese well in half horizontally. Place one half cut side up on a large round serving plate. Spread with walnut mixture, pressing down firmly. Top with second half, cut side down. Cover tightly with plastic wrap and refrigerate at least 5 hours. To serve, let torta come to room temperature and garnish with grape clusters.

LAYERED TACO SPREAD

1-⅓ c. refried beans (preferably homemade)
1-½ c. tomatillo sauce (or taco sauce)
⅔ c. sour cream
1 large ripe avocado, peeled, pitted and mashed
   with 2-3 tsp. lemon juice
2 medium size ripe tomatoes, diced and drained
½ to ⅔ c. finely chopped olives
6 green onions, white and 2 inches of green tops, finely minced
2 c. very finely shredded iceberg lettuce
¾ c. finely shredded Monterey Jack cheese
Tortilla chips

Combine beans with 1 cup of the tomatillo sauce, mix well, and spread in the center of a large round platter, making a round about 10 inches in diameter. Spread sour cream evenly over the bean mixture and then layer with remaining sauce, avocado mixture, tomatoes, olives, green onion, and lettuce. Sprinkle with cheese and serve with tortilla chips. About 30 servings.

SPINACH DIP

1 pkg. (10 oz.) frozen chopped spinach, thawed and drained
1 c. grated sharp cheddar cheese
1 pkg. Knorr's dry vegetable soup mix
2 c. sour cream   2 green onions, chopped
1 c. Hellman's mayo   1 round loaf rye bread

Mix all ingredients together for dip, cut out the center of the rye bread and fill the center with dip. Tear up remaining pieces of bread and arrange around the loaf of bread.

GARDEN VEGETABLE DIP

2 envelopes Lipton Spring Vegetable Cup-a-Soup
½ pint (8 oz.) sour cream or plain yogurt

In small bowl, blend cup-a-soup with sour cream; chill. Serve
with your favorite vegetables or chips. Makes about 1 cup dip.
Recipe can be doubled.

ITALIAN SHRIMP COCKTAIL

12 large butterfly shrimp, boiled and peeled
¾ c. ketchup
½ c. horseradish sauce (Heinz Sauce works)
1 tbsp. chili sauce   ½ tsp. basil

Mix cocktail sauce together. Arrange shrimp around bowl and
pour in cocktail sauce. Chill for 1 hour. Serve chilled.

KOOL-AID TWISTS

1 bag ready mix Kool-Aid   1 (32 oz.) can grapefruit juice
Mix together and serve chilled.

PARTY PUNCH

1 can (64 oz.) Hi-C fruit punch
1 liter ginger ale   1 jar (32 oz.) orange juice
½ gallon water, cooled   ½ gallon rainbow sherbet
1 bag ready mix Kool-Aid (cherry, strawberry, or fruit flavored)

Mix all ingredients together in punch bowl and add sherbet, stir.
Serve at room temperature.

CREAMY FRUIT DIP

1 (8 oz.) carton sour cream
2 tbsp. of flavored liqueur
1 tsp. brown sugar

Mix together in medium bowl. Chill for 1 hour. Serve with fresh fruit blocks, melon balls and berries.

MOCHA FONDUE

Makes 12 servings. Prep: 10 minutes. Cook: 15 minutes.

1 c. heavy cream
½ c. good-quality unsweetened cocoa powder
3 tbsp. freeze-dried instant coffee
2 tbsp. light corn syrup
12 oz. bittersweet chocolate, chopped granules
2 tbsp. coffee-flavored liqueur
½ tsp. cinnamon   ¼ c. milk (optional)
⅔ c. spring water   ⅔ c. sugar

In small bowl, whisk together cocoa powder, instant coffee, and cinnamon. In medium-size saucepan, stir together water, sugar and corn syrup. Bring to boiling; reduce heat and simmer, uncovered, until bubbly, slightly thickened and still clear, about 10 minutes. Remove saucepan from heat. Whisk in cocoa powder mixture. Return to heat. Stir in heavy cream. Bring to simmering over medium heat; simmer, uncovered, 5 minutes. Remove from heat. Stir in chopped chocolate and liqueur. For a thinner mixture if desired, stir in milk. Pour into fondue pot; keep warm over candle or canned heat burner. Serve with fruit and pound cake for dipping.

BRUSCHETTA

6 large tomatoes, chopped
2 tsp. sweet basil
2 cloves garlic, minced

1 c. olive oil
1 onion, finely chopped
Parmesan cheese (optional)

Mix together and serve on toast points.

SALSA DIP

Mix together 2 (8 oz.) pkgs. cream cheese, 1 c. salsa. Melt in microwave until bubbly. Olé!!

TACO DIP

Mix together 1 pkg. taco seasoning, 1 can refried beans, 1 c. shredded cheddar cheese, 1 c. sour cream, small minced onion. Can be served either hot or cold. Microwavable.

LEONARD'S PÂTÉ

1 tbsp. olive oil
1 pkg. turkey ham
2 onions
20 carrots

3 inch butter
1 pkg. chicken liver
25 mushrooms
2 zucchini

Cook over a medium high heat 15 to 20 minutes and blend.

Add:
1 tsp. grated nutmeg
3 envelopes, any Knox gelatin

1 tbsp. cracked peppercorn

Refrigerate in 2 loaf pans for 1 hour. Serve cold. Use within 7 days or freeze.

JOAN'S BROCCOLI BALLS

1 large onion, finely chopped
8 oz. Stove Top Stuffing (use canister)
20 oz. bag of frozen broccoli, chopped
½ Parmesan cheese   6 eggs
1 tsp. pepper   ½ tsp. red pepper
½ garlic salt   ¾ c. melted butter

Cook and drain broccoli. Mix all ingredients and refrigerate overnight. Roll into balls and bake at 350 degrees for 20 minutes.

RUSSIAN TEA

2 c. Tang   1 tbsp. cinnamon
2 c. sugar   1 tbsp. ground cloves
½ c. instant tea   1 pkg. lemonade mix

Mix all ingredients together. Use ½ tbsp. per 1 c. boiling water.

KEY LIME MARTINI

Equal parts Pineapple Juice, Lime Vodka, Vanilla Vodka, Plain Vodka, and half and half.

Splash of lime juice. Shake over ice and pour into martini glass.

NUTS & BERRIES

Pour the following over ice and stir.
2 shots Chambord liqueur
2 shots Frangelico liqueur
2 shots half & half

CURRIED MEAT BALLS

1 lb. ground beef
2 tsp. curry powder
1 c. stuffing mix

½ c. butter
½ tsp. salt
Freshly ground black pepper

Mix beef, curry powder, stuffing mix, salt, and pepper together. Shape into 32 small balls and sauté in butter over high heat for 5 minutes or until brown. Drain.

FRIED ZUCCHINI

3 small to medium sized zucchini, sliced diagonally
Dip zucchini in 1 beaten egg with 2 tbsp. water. Roll into flour mixture and fry in 1 stick butter and 2 cloves minced garlic.

Flour mixture:
½ c. flour
1 tsp. seasoned pepper

1 tbsp. seasoned salt
2 tbsp. cornmeal

FRIED BANANA PEPPERS

Split banana peppers, remove seed and fiber. Dip into beaten egg with 2 tbsp buttermilk. Roll into flour mixture and fry in hot cooking oil until golden brown.
Flour mixture:
½ c. flour
1 tsp. seasoned pepper

1 tsp. garlic salt
1 tsp. seasoned salt

STUFFED BANANA PEPPERS

6–8 hot or mild banana peppers, washed, cored & seeded
1 pkg. wonton wrappers   6–8 mozzarella string cheese sticks

Stuff peppers with cheese. Roll into wrappers baby diaper style and fry in hot vegetable oil. Serve with marinara sauce.

– 3 –

BREADS

NOTES

AMISH FRIENDSHIP BREAD

Day 1: receive bread starter
Day 2: stir once
Day 3: stir once
Day 4: stir once
Day 5: add 1 c. sugar, 1 c. flour, 1 c. milk
Day 6: stir once
Day 7: stir once
Day 8: stir once
Day 9: stir once
Day 10: add 1 c. sugar, 1 c. flour, 1 c. milk

Stir and put in large container.

After adding ingredients on day 10, stir well and place one cup of starter in 3 containers; to remaining batter add:

$\frac{1}{3}$ c. oil $\frac{1}{2}$ tsp. cinnamon
2 c. flour $\frac{1}{4}$ tsp. salt
1 c. sugar $\frac{1}{4}$ tsp. baking soda
3 eggs

Stir well and pour into 2 greased and sugared loaf pans. Bake at 350 degrees for 40 minutes. If you like moist, watch closely the last 5 minutes, take it out when toothpick comes out sticky but not quite clean. Fruit and or nuts may be added if desired. Give 1 container to friends or keep one for yourself to start again. Makes 2 loaves.

Starter:
1 c. sugar   1 c. flour
1 c. milk

BRAN MUFFINS

¼ c. oil
⅓ c. dark molasses or corn syrup
1–¼ c. buttermilk   3 c. whole bran cereal
2 egg whites, lightly beaten ½ c. raisins (optional)
1 c. sifted all-purpose flour 1 tsp. baking powder
¼ tsp. ground allspice ¼ to ⅓ c. light brown sugar

Sift together flour, baking powder, baking soda, allspice, and brown sugar. Combine oil, molasses, buttermilk, and eggs; beat until fluffy. Add dry ingredients, then add cereal and raisins. Grease and flour 24 muffin pans. Bake in preheated 350 degree oven for 15 to 20 minutes.

BEER MUFFINS

2 c. Bisquick
2 tbsp. sugar
½ (6 oz.) bottle beer

Combine all ingredients and beat for 30 seconds with mixer and pour into greased muffin pan. Bake at 425 degrees for 10 minutes.

DOUBLE QUICK ROLLS

2 pkgs. dry yeast   1 tsp. salt
2 tbsp sugar   2 eggs
1 c. warm water   2-¼ c. flour
2 tbsp shortening

Dissolve yeast and sugar in warm water. Stir in shortening, eggs and salt. Work in flour. Let dough rise 30 minutes. Punch down. Shape into rolls. Place on baking sheet and let rise 20-30 minutes. Bake at 400 degrees till golden brown.

BACON AND ONION MUFFINS

1 tbsp. Land-O-Lakes sweet cream butter
8 oz. (1 c.) Land-O-Lakes lean cream
½ tsp. salt   ¼ c. chopped onion
6 strips cooked, crumbled bacon
2 c. all-purpose flour   2 tbsp. sugar
⅓ c. milk   ½ tsp. baking powder
1 egg, beaten   ½ tsp. baking soda
Sesame seeds (optional)

Heat oven to 375 degrees. In 8" skillet melt butter. Stir in onion.
Cook over medium heat until tender (3-4 minutes); cool. In large
bowl combine flour, sugar, baking powder, baking soda, and
salt. In small bowl stir together onion, bacon, lean cream, milk,
and egg until blended well. Add to flour mixture, stirring just
enough to moisten. Spoon batter into greased 12 c. muffin pan.
Sprinkle with sesame seeds. Bake for 18 to 20 minutes or until
lightly browned. Serve warm with butter. Yield: 12 muffins.

ANGEL BISCUITS

2 pkgs. yeast   5 c. all purpose flour
¼ c. warm water   2 c. warm buttermilk
½ c. sugar   1 tbsp. baking powder
1 tbsp. salt   1 tsp. baking soda
1 c. shortening   melted butter

Dissolve yeast in warm water, let stand 5 minutes. Stir in buttermilk,
set aside. In large mixing bowl, stir dry ingredients; cut in shortening until mixture looks like coarse meal. Stir in yeast and milk.
Mix well. Turn onto floured bench. Knead lightly 4–5 times. Roll
out and cut in 1-in. pieces. Place on greased baking sheet and
let rise 1½–2 hours. Bake at 450° for 8–10 minutes. Baste with
melted butter.

IDY MAE'S SOUR DOUGH BREAD

Must be fed every 3-9 days to keep alive.

Feed Starter:

1 c. warm water   ½ c. potato flakes
1 c. flour   ½ c. sugar

Let this sit in warm place with lid on tightly overnight. In the morning save 1 generous cut of starter; put in a jar; cover tightly and refrigerate. Put the rest of the starter in a large bowl and add:

½ c. sugar   2 tsp. salt
½ c. warm water   6 to 7-½ c. flour
½ oil

Mix until stiff. Let rise 6-8 hours. Knead lightly. Shape into loaves or rolls. Grease pan.

For Bread:
Let rise 4 or more hours, cook at 350 degrees for 30 minutes.

For Rolls:
Let rise 2-4 hours, bake at 350 degrees for 20 minutes.

Flour:
Use ½ c. wheat germ for ¼ c. of flour, or 1 full cup of wheat flour in place of 1 c. of white flour.

For Sweet Rolls:
Press out on cookie sheet lightly. Use sugar and cinnamon to taste, sprinkle lightly. Roll up and cut into desired size.

For Hamburger Buns:
Just make rolls extra large and bake on cookie sheet.

When you add the first ingredients to the starter, you can dump everything into a large jar and stir.

AUNT JUANITA BLACKBURN'S MEXICAN CORNBREAD

1 c. yellow cornmeal (not self-rising)

½ Wesson oil
1 c. chopped onion
1 c. grated cheese
1 chopped Jalapeno pepper
½ can cream style corn
¾ c. milk

1 c. flour
¼ sugar
4 tsp. baking powder
½ tsp. salt
2 eggs

Mix together as given above and turn into greased skillet. Bake at 425 degrees for 20 to 30 minutes or until golden brown. Makes a big loaf.

DOUBLE QUICK DINNER ROLLS

1 c. warm water
1 tsp. salt
1-¼ c. flour
¼ c. soft shortening

1 pkg. dry yeast
¼ c. sugar
1 egg

Dissolve yeast in warm water, add sugar and salt; let set until small bubbles come to the top. Add about half of the flour and mix thoroughly. Add egg, shortening, and rest of flour and mix well. Turn onto floured counter top and knead until smooth—about 3 minutes. Put into a large, well-greased bowl and turn to grease top of the dough. Cover with a clean towel and let rise in a warm place for about 1 hour or until double in bulk. Return to floured counter and knead until all air bubbles are gone. Make into desired rolls, cover with a towel, and put in warm place to rise until double in bulk. Bake at 400 degrees until golden brown. Makes one dozen rolls.

For whole wheat rolls: Use ¾ cup wheat flour and 1-½ cups white flour. Give whole wheat rolls 10 to 15 minutes longer rising time as the whole wheat is a heavier dough.

"ENI'S" ZUCCHINI BREAD

3 c. flour
1-½ tsp. cinnamon
3 eggs
2 tsp. vanilla
1 (8 oz.) can drained pineapple

2 c. sugar
¾ c. chopped nuts
1 c. oil
2 c. shredded zucchini

Cream together sugar and oil until fluffy, then add eggs and vanilla. Stir in flour and cinnamon until well mixed. Next add zucchini, nuts, and pineapple. Pour into 2 greased and floured loaf pans and bake for 1 hour at 350 degrees.

AUNT LORETTA'S BOHEMIAN BRAID

Mix together:
2 c. lukewarm milk   2 tsp. salt
¾ c. sugar

Soak 5 minutes and mix in:
2 pkgs. dry yeast   ¼ c. warm water

Stir in:
2 eggs
½ c. shortening (¼ c. butter, ¼ c. Crisco)

Mix in about ¼ of flour with spoon, the remaining with hand: 7-½ to 8 cups flour (sifted)

After mixing mixture with hand until dough pulls away from bowl, sprinkle flour on board and knead until smooth, adding flour if needed. Place dough in well greased bowl, turning so top of dough is greased. Cover with damp warm cloth and let stand in warm (75° to 85°) place for 1-½ to 2 hours or until doubled in size. Press two fingers in dough, if indentation is left, dough is doubled. Punch down and turn over, let rise about 45 minutes more. The warmer the place the less rising time required.

After second rising, have ready and knead in:

2 tsp. grated lemon rind   ½ c. raisins
⅛ tsp. mace   1 c. chopped or slivered blanched
almonds

Divide dough into two equal parts. Lay one part aside. Take the other part and divide into 4 equal parts. Take 3 of these parts and braid loosely. I begin in the middle, turn around and braid to the other end. Now take the remaining 4th part and divide into 3 parts. Braid this as before, place on top of large braid and seal ends of small braid into larger braid. Let rise 50 to 60 minutes. Repeat with other part. Bake at 350 degrees 40 to 50 minutes. Cool. Decorate with icing.

Confectioner's sugar icing, mix together:
1 c. sifted confectioner's sugar
½ tsp. lemon juice with some grated lemon rind
1-½ tbsp. warm milk

Spread over braid. Decorate with pecan halves and green and red candied cherries.

This dough can be used for other yeast breads, such as doughnuts, cinnamon rolls, rolls (by decreasing sugar to ½ to ⅔ cups).

BAKING POWDER BISCUITS WITH CHIVES

2 c. sifted flour   ½ c. shortening
1 tbsp. double-acting baking powder
⅔ c. milk   ¼ c. chopped chives
1 tsp. salt

Sift flour with baking powder and salt. Cut in shortening with a pastry blender until the mixture resembles coarse meal. Add milk and chives, stirring until a soft dough is formed. Knead gently on a lightly floured board for 30 seconds. Roll or pat dough ½ inch thick. Cut into 12 biscuits. Bake on a baking sheet in a hot oven (425 degrees) for 15 minutes.

SPOON BREAD

1 c. white corn meal
2 qt. milk
2 tbsp. butter

4 eggs, well beaten
¼ tsp. salt

Scald milk in the top of a double boiler. Place over hot water, stir in corn meal, butter and salt. Cook for 15 minutes or until thickened, stirring frequently. Pour in beaten eggs, stire, and bake in a greased casserole in a hot oven (400 degrees) for 45 minutes. Serves 6

STACY MCCOY'S WHOLE WHEAT BREAD

For bread machine lovers.

1-⅝ c. water
⅜ c. whole wheat flour
3 tbsp. sugar
1-½ tbsp. dry milk

2-⅝ c. bread flour
1-½ tsp. salt
1-½ tsp. butter
3 tbsp. dry yeast

Set bread machine on selection for wheat!!! YUMMY!!!

– 4 –

DESSERTS

NOTES

HOMEMADE REESE CUPS

2 c. peanut butter, creamy or crunchy
2 c. confectioner's sugar

Mix thoroughly until crumbly. Roll into balls and pat into cup shapes. Dip in 1 block semi-sweet chocolate mixed with 1 oz. Gulfwax. Lay out on wax paper until chocolate has set. Then chill until ready to eat.

PRETZEL SALAD

9-½ oz. bag pretzels, crushed
1 c. sugar   2 sticks butter, melted

Mix well and press together in bottom of glass plan.

2 tbsp. cornstarch
1 can crushed pineapple, drained, reserving juice

Drain pineapple and set aside.
Mix pineapple juice and cornstarch together and cook until thickened. Add pineapple.

1 box jello, your choice.

Mix jello according to package directions, add pineapple. Chill until set. Spread over the pretzel crust. Mix up 1 package Dream Whip (mix according to package directions). Mix together 1 (8 oz.) package cream cheese and ½ cup sugar and the Dream Whip. Spread over the top of the jello mixture. Let set overnight.

BLONDE BROWNIES

1-½ c. sifted all-purpose flour   ¾ c. brown sugar, firmly packed
½ tsp. baking powder   1 c. sugar
½ tsp. salt   2 eggs
½ c. butter   1 tsp. vanilla
1 bag bits o brickle

Sift flour, salt, and baking powder together. Cream butter with
both sugars, add eggs, and vanilla. Beat until fluffy. Blend in dry
ingredients. Stir in bits o brickle. Spread evenly in well greased
9" x 12" pan. Bake at 350 degrees for 30 minutes. Cool and cut
into bars.

**The next four recipes were given to me by my Dad, Leonard
McCoy, the best hillbilly chef in the state of Kentucky.**

BANANA'S TAB

½ stick butter, melted   2 tbsp. brown sugar
Juice from 1 orange   2 tbsp. grated orange rind
½ c. white wine   2 large bananas

Dissolve sugar in butter and bring to a boil. Add juice of 1 orange
and 2 tbsp. grated orange rind, ½ c. white wine and simmer. Split
2 large bananas down the middle and then cut into thirds. Sauté
bananas in hot mixture for 1 minute; spoon over vanilla ice cream
and serve.

MACADAMIA NUT PIE

Filling:
In double boiler, place 3 egg yolks, 2-½ c. milk, 1 c. sugar. Stir 2 tbsp. cornstarch with 2 tbsp. hot water; add to egg yolk mixture, bring to boil, stirring constantly with wire whisk. Cook until thickened. Cool. Add 1 tsp. vanilla. Crush 1 jar of macadamia nuts, reserving 8 nuts. Add crushed nuts to filling. Beat 1 pint whipping cream, stiff, reserve ½ cup. Fold the remaining into the filling. In double boiler, melt a block Baker's Semi-Sweet German Chocolate. Reserving 3 tbsp. in small bowl. Spread melted chocolate onto cooled baked pie crust; top with ½ cup of reserved whipped cream, and place chocolate covered with nuts on top.

PUMPKIN SOUFFLÉ PIE

2 c. fresh pumpkin, cooked	½ c. sugar
¼ c. molasses or ½ c. brown sugar	
¼ tsp. allspice	¼ tsp. cinnamon
¼ tsp. ginger	¼ nutmeg
2 eggs, beaten	½ c. heavy cream

Stir all ingredients together, well. Bake at 450 degrees for 15 minutes; reduce heat to 350 degrees and bake for 45 minutes. Use homemade pie crust for Pillsbury All-Ready pie crust.

Canned pumpkin may be used.

FRESH COCONUT CREAM PIE

1 large coconut, drill hole in the eye and drain milk.

Bake coconut, in shell in 400 degree oven until cracked. Remove from oven and cool. With a hammer, crack and peel coconut. Place in food processor and chop.

Filling:
In double boiler, place 3 eggs, 2-½ c. milk. 1 c. sugar*, mix 2 tbsp. cornstarch with 2 tbsp. hot water, and add to egg mixture. Bring to boil and cook until thickened. Cool and add 1 tsp. vanilla and 1 cup coconut. Pour into baked pie shell. Top with meringue and brown until golden brown.

Meringue:
6 egg whites   1 c. confectioner's sugar
Beat until stiff and add 1 tsp. vanilla.

*If using canned coconut only ½ cup sugar is needed.

APPLE STREUSEL PIE

1–9" pie shell, unbaked (Pillsbury)
2 tbsp. butter or margarine, melted
3 all-purpose apples, peeled, pared and thinly sliced
1 (28 oz.) jar mincemeat   3 tbsp. unsifted flour
Streusel topping

Preheat oven to 425 degrees. In a large bowl, toss apples with flour and butter. Arrange in pie shell. Top with mincemeat and streusel topping. Bake 10 minutes, then reduce heat to 375 degrees. Continue baking for 25 minutes. Cool slightly and serve warm.

Streusel Topping:
Combine in a bowl, ½ cup unsifted flour, ¼ cup firmly packed brown sugar, 1 teaspoon ground cinnamon. Cut in ⅓ cup cold margarine until crumbly, add ½ cup chopped nuts.

APPLE CUSTARD PIE

1 c. sugar
1 (8 oz.) carton lean cream
2 eggs, beaten
2 tbsp. flour
¼ tsp. salt
1 tsp. vanilla

3 c. peeled and chopped apples
9" unbaked pie shell (Pillsbury)
3 tbsp. butter
¼ c. flour
¼ c. firmly packed brown sugar

Preheat oven to 375 degrees.

In a large bowl combine white sugar, lean cream, eggs, 2 tbsp. flour, salt, and vanilla. Stir in apples. Pour in pie shell. In a qt. saucepan melt butter, stir in ¼ c. flour and brown sugar. Crumble over pie. Bake for 35 to 45 minutes or until filling is set. Cool completely and store in refrigerator. If crust gets too brown while baking, cover with foil.

CREAMY FRUIT SALAD

6 c. assorted fresh fruit sliced or chopped
1 box instant Jello pudding (vanilla)
1 bag frozen berries

Stir fruit together, sprinkle pudding over top and mix with spoon.

BANANA DELIGHT

2 bags frozen raspberries   5 bananas
1 (4 oz.) box vanilla instant pudding

Mix all ingredients and chill 2 hours.

RONNIE'S FAVORITE QUICK FRUIT DESSERT

1 can fruit cocktail
4 fresh peaches, peeled and chopped
2 apples, peeled and chopped
1 c. fruit juice (orange)   ½ c. cornstarch

Mix fruit together in a large bowl. Cook cornstarch and juice over medium heat until boiling and boil 5 minutes, stirring constantly. Cool and pour over fruit.

Serve with Pirouette Cookies.

JOAN'S PEANUT BUTTER DREAM BARS

2 c. quick oats, uncooked   1 c. brown sugar, firmly packed
1-½ c. all-purpose flour   1 c. chopped peanuts
½ tsp. baking soda   ¾ tsp. salt
1 c. margarine
1 can Eagle Brand Cream, condensed milk
⅓ c. peanut butter   1 c. M & M's plain candies

Combine flour, oats, peanuts, sugar, baking soda, and salt; mix well. Add margarine; mix until dry ingredients are thoroughly moistened and mixture resembles coarse crumbs. Reserve 1-½ cups crumb mixture; press remaining mixture onto bottom of greased 15½" x 10½" jelly roll pan. Bake at 375 degrees for 12 minutes. Combine condensed milk and peanut butter in small bowl, mixing until well blended. Spread over partially baked crust to within ¼" from edge. Combine reserved crumb mixture and candies; sprinkle evenly over condensed milk mixture, pressing in lightly. Continue to bake for 20 to 22 minutes or until golden brown. Cool and cut into bars.

BANANA SPLIT CAKE

3 c. or 1 box of graham cracker crumbs
1 large can crushed pineapple, drained
2 sticks butter, softened   1 large container Cool Whip
2 eggs   1 jar maraschino cherries
2 c. confectioners sugar   3 or 4 large bananas
1 pkg. chopped pecans, about 1-½ c.

Mix graham cracker crumbs as directed on box for pie crust and place in bottom of an oblong glass baking dish. Press down good. Beat for 15 minutes: butter, sugar, and eggs. Pour over graham crust. Cover with sliced bananas and crushed pineapples, top with Cool Whip, add finely chopped nut and cherries cut in half. Refrigerate for 2 hours.

PINEAPPLE CREAM PUDDING

½ c. flaked coconut   1-½ c. milk
⅔ c. flour   1 (8 oz.) can crushed pineapple
⅔ c. plus ½ c. sugar   2 tsp. vanilla
4 eggs, separated   ¼ tsp. cream of tarter
2–⅛ tsp. salt

Put half the coconut in 6 (4 oz.) ramekins or custard cups. In a medium saucepan, combine flour, ⅔ cup of the sugar and ⅛ tsp. salt. Whisk in the yolks. Add the milk gradually. Cook over medium heat, stirring until thick—6 to 8 minutes. Drain pineapple and stir in with 1 tsp. vanilla. Pour in custard cups. Beat egg whites until frothy, add cream of tarter and ⅛ tsp. salt and beat until whites hold soft peaks. Gradually beat in ½ cup of the sugar until meringue hold stiff peaks. Beat in 1 tsp. vanilla. Spoon meringue onto pudding. Sprinkle tops with remaining ¼ cup coconut. Bake in 350 degree oven until golden brown, about 15 minutes.

FUN & QUICK PEANUT BUTTER SQUARES

¼ c. brown sugar, firmly packed
¼ c. salted cocktail nuts   ½ c. corn syrup
3-½ c. Kellogg's Honey & Nut Corn Flakes
½ c. peanut butter   ¼ c. seedless raisins

Measure sugar, corn syrup, and peanut butter into large saucepan. Cook over medium heat, stirring constantly until peanut butter melts and mixture is well blended. Remove from heat. Add raisins, cocktail nuts, and cereal, mixing until well coated. Press into buttered 8" x 8" x 2" pan. Bake at 350 degrees for 25 minutes or until golden brown. Cut into squares. Makes 16 bars.

CREAMY CHEESE PIE

1 pkg. (8 oz.) cream cheese, softened
1 tsp. vanilla   ⅓ c. sugar
1 container (4 oz.) Cool Whip, thawed
½ c. sour cream   Crunchy crumb crust

Beat cheese until smooth. Gradually beat in sugar. Blend in sour cream and vanilla; fold in Cool Whip. Spoon into crunch crumb crust. Chill until set, at least 3 hours. Served topped with sweetened fresh fruit, if desired.

CRUNCHY CRUMB CRUST

Combine 1-½ c. Post Grape-Nuts cereal and ⅓ c. sugar in electric blender. Blend at high speed, turning blender off rapidly 3 times or until cereal forms coarse crumbs. Pour in 9-inch pie pan. Add ⅓ c. butter or margarine, melted, and mix well; press firmly on the bottom and sides of the pan. Chill for 1 hour. (Or bake at 375 degrees for 5 to 8 minutes, or until lightly browned, cool.)

ELSIE'S MAGIC PIE

¼ c. lemon juice   11 oz. can crushed pineapple
8 oz. Cool Whip   11 oz. can mandarin oranges
1 can Eagle Brand condensed milk
small jar maraschino cherries

Drain fruit well. Stir juice, milk, and Cool Whip. Fold fruit mixture together. Chill. Add coconut if desired. Use store bought crust.

SISTER DICKEY'S ORANGE MOLD

1 large box orange Jello   8 oz. container of Cool Whip
1 medium container cottage cheese
1 can mandarin oranges

Mix together and chill for 12 hours.

ORANGE PARFAIT

large container Cool Whip   ½ c. coconut
1 c. mini marshmallows   ½ c. chopped pecans
8 oz. cream cheese (softened)   1 small box orange jello
1 can fruit cocktail

Mix together and chill for 12 hours.

CHOCOLATE MOCHA MACAROON BUNDT CAKE

1 pkg. chocolate macaroon cake mix

Filling:

⅓ c. water   1 tsp. instant coffee granules

Cake:

1-¼ c. water   2 eggs
¼ c. butter or margarine, softened
¾ c. miniature chocolate chips
1 tsp. instant coffee granule

Glaze:

5 tsp. water   ½ tsp. instant coffee granules

Heat oven to 350 degrees. Flour and grease a 12-cup bundt pan. In small bowl, blend clear packet of filling mix with remaining filling ingredients until smooth. Set aside. In large bowl, combine cake mix packet with remaining cake ingredients, except chocolate chips, until moistened. Stir in chips; mix well. Pour evenly into prepared pan. Spoon prepared filling mix in narrow ring over center of batter. Filling should not touch sides of the pan. Bake at 350 degrees for 35 to 45 minutes or until toothpick comes out clean. Cool upright in pan for 25 minutes; invert into serving plate. Cool completely. In small bowl, dissolve coffee in water, blend in glaze mix until smooth. If thinner glaze is desired, stir in additional water, a few drops at a time. Spoon over top of cake, allowing some to run down the sides of the cake. Garnish as desired. Store loosely covered. Makes 16 servings.

CHOCOLATE CHIP COOKIES

2 c. flour
1 c. sugar
½ c. light brown sugar
2 eggs

1 c. shortening
2 tsp. baking powder
1 bag chocolate chips
1 c. chopped nuts (optional)

Stir together all ingredients, add chips and nuts and mix with a spoon. Drop by rounded spoonfuls onto a well-greased cookie sheet.

Bake in a 350 degree oven for 8 to 10 minutes.

PECAN COOKIES

1-½ c. sifted flour
½ tsp. baking soda
½ tsp. salt
½ butter
¾ firmly packed brown sugar

1 egg
1 tsp. vanilla
1 bag bits o brickle
½ chopped pecans

Combine flour, baking soda, and salt. Cream butter with sugar, add egg and vanilla. Mix until creamy. Stir in dry ingredients, blend in brickle and nuts. Drop by spoonfuls onto greased cookie sheet. Bake at 350 degrees for 10 to 12 minutes. Remove from sheet and cool.

RED VELVET CAKE

1 tsp. vanilla
½ margarine
1-½ c. sugar
2 eggs

2 tsp. cocoa
2 oz. red food coloring
1 tsp. vinegar

Blend all above ingredients, add:
1 tsp. baking soda
2 c. cake flour

1 c. buttermilk

Bake at 350 degrees for 35 to 40 minutes. Cool on wire rack. This cake presents itself as a good Christmas dessert. Bake in 2 round pans.

CREAM CHEESE ICING

1 8 oz. package cream cheese, softened
1 tsp. vanilla
1 box confectioner's sugar

1 stick butter, softened

Mix well in mixer on low speed, adding 1 tsp. vanilla, and 1 box confectioner's sugar.

Add: 1 c. chopped nuts (optional)

CHEWY BROWNIES

½ c. butter (1 stick)   1 tsp. vanilla
4 oz. (4 squares) unsweetened chocolate
2 c. all-purpose flour (less 2 tbsp.)
4 eggs at room temperature
1 c. chopped pecans, English walnuts or black walnuts
¼ tsp. salt

Heat oven to 350 degrees. Grease a 13" x 9" x 2" pan. Carefully melt butter and chocolate in a heavy saucepan over low heat. Remove from heat and cool. Beat eggs and salt until frothy, add vanilla. Add sugar ½ cut at a time. Beat well. Stir in the chocolate mixture. When mixture has a well-marbled appearance, fold in flour. Add nuts. Spread evenly in well-greased pan and bake for 30 minutes. Remove from oven and cool before cutting.

MAPLE FROSTING

¼ c. Crisco shortening or butter (if using butter, add 3 tbsp. milk)
½ tsp. salt   2 tsp. vanilla
⅓ c. maple syrup   3 c. confectioner's sugar

Combine Crisco, salt, syrup, vanilla, and 1 c. of the sugar. Mix until smooth. Add remaining sugar and milk alternately. Mix until creamy. Add more sugar to thicken or milk to thin.

BUTTER CREAM FROSTING

4 tbsp. flour	1 c. milk

Mix together in saucepan. Cook over medium heat until it thickens. Remove from heat and cool.

¾ c. shortening	1 tsp. vanilla
¼ c. butter	1 c. confectioner's sugar

Beat until fluffy, add thickened mixture and beat for 20 minutes. If icing will not hold a toothpick in top of bowl ½ inserted then beat 5 more minutes, adding one more cup of sugar as needed.

HEATH BRICK 'N' PECAN COOKIES

1-½ c. sifted flour	1 egg
½ tsp baking soda	1 tsp. vanilla
½ tsp. salt	1 bag Bits 'O' Brickle
½ c. butter	⅓ c. chopped pecans
¾ c. brown sugar	

Combine flour, baking soda, and salt—sift together. Cream butter with brown sugar. Add egg and vanilla; mix until smooth and creamy. Stir in dry ingredients; blend in Bit 'O' Brickle and pecans. Drop by tablespoons 2 inches apart onto greased baking sheets. Bake in 350 degree oven 10 to 12 minutes. Remove from baking sheets immediately, cool on rack. Yield: about 3 dozen cookies.

HEATH BRICKLE BLONDE BROWNIES

1-½ c. sifted flour
1 tsp. baking powder
½ tsp. salt
½ c. butter
1 c. sugar

1 c. brown sugar, packed
2 eggs
1 tsp. vanilla
1 bag Bits 'O' Brickle

Sift flour, baking powder, and salt together. Cream butter with both sugars, add eggs and vanilla; beat until fluffy. Blend in dry ingredients. Stir in Bits 'O' Brickle. Spread evenly in well-greased 9" x 12" baking pan. Bake at 350 degrees for 30 minutes. When cool, cut into bars 3" x 1". If desired, when cool, frost with white or chocolate butter frosting. Makes 3 dozen blonde brownies.

AUNT OLA MAE'S APPLE CRISP CAKE

3 eggs
2 c. sugar
1-½ c. oil
3 c. chopped raw apples

1 c. nuts
2 tsp. vanilla
3 c. flour
1 tsp. baking soda

Mix well and bake for 1-½ hours at 325 degrees in greased tube pan.

*Black walnuts are especially good in this cake.

CHOCOLATE MERINGUE BARS

1 pkg. Pillsbury Chocolate Cake Mix
2 egg whites   ¼ tsp. cream of tartar
⅓ c. water   ¼ c. sugar
¼ c. butter, softened   ½ c. chocolate chips
2 egg yolks, reserve whites   ¼ c. chopped pecans

Heat oven to 350 degrees. In large bowl, combine cake mix, water, butter, and egg yolks at low speed until moistened; beat 1 minute at medium speed. Butter will be thick. Spread in ungreased 13" x 9" pan. In small bowl, combine egg whites, and cream of tarter, beat until foamy. Gradually add sugar, beating until stiff peaks form, about 3 minutes. Spread evenly over base. Sprinkle with chocolate chips and pecans. Bake at 350 degrees for 30 to 40 minutes or until meringue is light golden brown. Cool completely, cut into bars. Makes 36 bars.

BELVA HAGER'S CREAM PULL CANDY

3 c. sugar   ½ stick butter or margarine
1 c. warm water   2 tsp. vanilla
½ c. cream

Cook and stir ingredients together until boiling fast. Then absolutely no more stirring. Cook to 260 degrees on candy thermometer. Pour out on a meat dish that has been buttered and put in freezer. Spread 2 tsp. vanilla on top of candy and put in refrigerator. Keep pulling sides of candy as it cools. When it is cool enough, lift candy from meat dish and pull. With buttered scissors, pull and cut.

STRAWBERRIES WITH ZABAGLIONE

1 pkg. Pepperidge Farm pastry shells
1-¼ c. sliced fresh strawberries
¼ c. granulated sugar
¼ c. Marsala wine   3 egg yolks

Prepare pastry shells according to package directions. When cool, fill with sliced strawberries. In the top of a double boiler beat egg yolks, sugar, and wine over simmering water with an electric mixer for 5 to 7 minutes until foamy and very thick. Do not overcook or mixture will curdle. Pour over berries in shells and serve immediately. Serves 6.

MAE ETTA PRESTON'S MEXICAN FRUIT CAKE

2 tsp. baking soda
2 c. sugar   2 c. flour
2 eggs   1 c. chopped pecans
20 oz. can crushed pineapple with syrup
1 jar chopped maraschino cherries, chopped and drained

Mix all ingredients together and pour in a 9"x13" greased and floured pan. Bake at 350 degrees for 45 minutes. Prepare frosting while cake is baking:

Frosting:
8 oz. cream cheese   2 c. powdered sugar
1 tsp. vanilla   1 stick butter, room temperature

Blend cream cheese and butter until creamy, add vanilla and sugar. Frost cake as soon as it comes out of oven. Eat hot or cold.

CAROLERS COOKIES

1 c. margarine
1 c. sugar
2 eggs
½ tsp. vanilla
3-½ c. flour
½ tsp. baking powder

½ tsp. baking soda
½ tsp. salt
2 c. sifted confectioner's sugar
3 tbsp. milk
Food coloring
Jets marshmallows

Cream margarine and sugar until light and fluffy. Blend in eggs and vanilla. Add combined dry ingredients; mix well. Chill. Roll dough out on lightly floured surface to ⅛ inch thickness, cut with 3 inch assorted cutters. Place on greased cookie sheets. Bake at 400 degrees, 6 to 8 minutes or until edges are lightly browned. Cool.

Combine confectioner's sugar and milk; mix well. Tint as desired with food coloring. Frost cookies. To use marshmallows for decorating, cut across the flat side using scissors dipped in water. Dip cut sides into decorative candies or sugars. Place on cookies with assorted candies to form designs. Makes about 4 dozen cookies.

FLOURLESS CHOCOLATE ALMOND CAKE

8 oz. semi-sweet chocolate
2 oz. unsweetened chocolate
¾ c. butter
1 c. plus 2 tbsp sugar

6 eggs separated
1 tsp. vanilla
1 c. ground almonds
1 c. heavy cream

Heat oven to 350 degrees. Butter a deep 9" cake pan and line bottom with buttered wax paper. Melt chocolate in double boiler and let cool. Cream butter with ¾ cup sugar. Beat in egg yolks, one by one. Stir in chocolate, vanilla, and almonds. Beat egg whites and salt to soft peaks. Gradually beat in ¼ cup sugar until whites hold stiff peaks. Stir ⅓ of egg whites into chocolate mixture. Fold into remaining egg whites. Pour into pan and bake until a toothpick inserted in the middle comes out with moist crumbs, 35 to 40 minutes. Let cake cool in pan. Whip cream with 2 tbsp. sugar. Serve cake with whipped cream and berries if desired.

FESTIVE FANTASY FUDGE

3 c. sugar
¾ c. margarine
⅔ c. evaporated milk
12 oz. pkg. semi-sweet chocolate pieces
1 tsp. vanilla

7 oz. jar marshmallow cream
3-½ oz. can flaked coconut
½ c. silvered toasted almonds

Combine sugar, margarine, and milk in heavy 2-½ quart saucepan; bring to full rolling boil, stirring constantly. Combine to boil for 5 minutes, stirring constantly to prevent sticking. Remove from heat, stir in chocolate pieces until melted. Add marshmallow cream, coconut, almonds, and vanilla; beat until well blended. Pour into greased 13"x9" pan. Cool at room temperature; cut into squares. Makes about 3 pounds.

GRASSHOPPER ICE CREAM PIE

1 pint vanilla ice cream, softened
2 tbsp. lemon juice
2 tbsp. white cream de. cacao*
2 tbsp. green crème de menthe*
3 c. whipped topping, thawed
9 inch chocolate crumb pie crust

*Or use 6 drops of green food coloring, 1 tsp. vanilla and ¼ tsp. peppermint extract.

Combine ice cream, lemon juice, crème de menthe and crème de cacao in bowl. Fold in whipped topping, blending well. Freeze, if necessary, until mixture will mound. Spoon into crust. Freeze until firm, at least 4 hours. Garnish with chocolate curls, if desired. Store leftovers in freezer.

STRAWBERRY SHORTCUT

1 (10-¾ oz.) pound cake
1 pint strawberries, sliced, and sweetened*
1-¾ c. (4 oz.) whipped topping, thawed
*Or use 2 c. sliced peaches

Cut cake into 12 pieces. Place 6 of the slices on a large serving plate or 6 individual dessert plates. Arrange half of the strawberries on cake slices; spread with half of the whipped topping. Repeat layers, ending with a dollop of whipped topping. Makes 6 servings.

FROZEN STRAWBERRY YOGURT PIE

2 container (8 oz. each) vanilla yogurt
3-½ whipped topping, thawed
2 c. sweetened diced, sliced or finely chopped strawberries
9-inch graham cracker crust

Fold yogurt into whipped topping, blend well, fold in strawberries. Spoon into crust. Freeze until firm, 4 hours or overnight. Remove from freezer 30 minutes before service and keep chilled in refrigerator. Garnish with additional whole strawberries if desired. Store any leftovers in freezer.

FROZEN PEANUT BUTTER PIE

1 (8 oz.) pkg. cream cheese, softened
1 (14 oz) can Eagle Brand sweetened condensed milk
¾ c. peanut butter   2 tbsp lemon juice
1 tsp. vanilla
1 c. whipping cream or 4 oz. container whipped topping
Chocolate fudge ice cream topping
1 chocolate crunch crust

In large mixer bowl, beat cheese until fluffy, gradually beat in Eagle Brand then peanut butter until smooth. Stir in lemon juice and vanilla. Fold in whipped cream. Turn into prepared crust. Drizzle topping over pie. Freeze for 4 hours or until firm. Return leftover to freezer.

Chocolate Crunch Crust:
In heavy saucepan, over low heat, melt $1/3$ cup margarine or butter and 1 (6 oz.) package semi-sweet chocolate chips. Remove from heat; gently stir in 2-½ cups oven toasted rice cereal until completely coated. Press on bottom and up side of buttered 9-inch or 10-inch pie plate. Chill 30 minutes.

BLACKBERRY COBBLER

Filling:
2-½ c. fresh blackberries, washed
½ stick butter, cut into pats
2 c. sugar   1 tsp. ground allspice

Crust:
2 c. sifted self-rising flour   ¼ tsp. salt
½ c. Crisco shortening   1 tsp. sugar
½ c. ice water

Place flour, salt, and sugar in a large bowl. Cut shortening into flour until well crumbled adding ice water a little at a time. Roll out thin on a well-floured bench and fit-cut enough crust to cover a 9-inch by 13-inch casserole dish. Fill with berry filling and cut strips of crust for top. Arrange into a checkered pattern. Bake at 350 degrees for 30 to 40 minutes.

FRUIT BOWL SUPREME

1 can mandarin orange sections, well drained*
1 can (8-¼ oz.) crushed pineapple in syrup, well drained
3 c. (8 oz.) whipped topping
2 c. coconut
2 c. miniature marshmallows
½ c. milk
*Or use 1 can (16 oz.) fruit cocktail in place of oranges, well drained.

Combine all ingredients, mixing well. Chill about 1 hour. Serve as dessert or as salad on crisp salad greens, if desired. Makes 6 cups or 12 servings.

CHOCOLATE RASPBERRY BUNDT CAKE

1 pkg. Tunnel of Fudge cake mix
10 oz. pkg. frozen raspberries, thawed and drained, reserving liquid

Filling:
¼ c. reserved raspberry liquid   ¼ c. oil

Cake:
1-¼ c. water   3 eggs
¼ c. oil

Glaze:
1 c. whipping cream   Drained raspberries

Heat oven to 350 degrees. Grease and flour 12 cup bundt pan. In small bowl, blend small clear packet of filling mix with remaining filling ingredients until smooth, set a side. In large bowl, combine large clear packet of cake mix with remaining cake ingredients at low speed until moistened, beat 2 minutes at medium speed. Pour evenly into prepared pan. Spoon prepared filling evenly in narrow ring over center of cake batter, not allowing filling to touch the sides of the pan. Bake at 350 degrees for 35 to 45 minutes or until toothpick comes out clean. Cool upright in pan for 45 minutes; invert onto serving plat. Cool completely. Dust with powdered sugar, if desired. In small bowl, beat whipping cream and glaze mix until stiff; fold in drained raspberries. To serve, top individual slices of cake with topping. Makes 16 servings. Store cake loosely covered.

CHOCOLATE MOUSSE RUM BUNDT CAKE

1 pkg. Chocolate Mousse cake mix

Filling:

¾ c. water   Small clear packet filling mix

Cake:

¾ c. water   ¼ c. rum
¼ c. oil   3 eggs
¾ c. chocolate chips

Glaze:

¼ c. chocolate chips   1 tbsp. rum
1 tsp. water

Heat oven to 350 degrees. Grease and flour 12 cup bundt pan. In small bowl, blend small clear packet of filling mix, and half of water until smooth. Stir in remaining water; mix well. Set aside for 10 minutes. In large bowl, combine clear packet of cake mix and remaining cake ingredients except chocolate chips at low speed until moistened. Stir in chocolate chips; mix well. Pour half of batter into prepared pan, spread evenly. Spoon prepared filling evenly in narrow ring over center of cake batter. Filling should not touch sides of pan. Spoon remaining cake batter over filling. Bake at 350 degrees for 40 to 50 minutes or until toothpick comes out clean. In small saucepan, combine glaze ingredients over low heat until chips are melted, stirring occasionally. Cool glaze drizzle over top of cake. Garnish as desired. Store loosely covered. Makes 16 servings.

CHOCOLATE PECAN BARS

Cream 1 cup butter or margarine and $\frac{1}{3}$ cup firmly packed brown sugar. Add 2 cups unsifted flour and beat until crumbly. Press into bottom of 13" x 9" pan. Bake at 350 degrees for 20 minutes, or until lightly browned. Meanwhile melt 3 tbsp. butter or margarine and 1 pkg. (4 oz.) Baker's German sweet chocolate over low heat. Combine 3 slightly beaten eggs, 1 cup light corn syrup, $\frac{1}{3}$ cup light brown sugar, 1 tsp. vanilla, and chocolate mixture; mix well. Stir in 1 cup chopped pecans and 1 cup Baker's angel flake coconut. Pour over hot crust. Bake 35 to 40 minutes longer or until top is puffed. Makes about 4 dozen.

GRAND MARNIER BUNDT CAKE

1 pkg. Bundt Boston Cream cake mix
11 oz. can mandarin oranges, chopped, and well drained, reserving liquid

Filling:
$\frac{1}{3}$ c. water   2 tbsp. oil
2 tbsp. Grand Marnier or other orange flavored liqueur

Cake:
$\frac{1}{2}$ c. flour $\frac{1}{3}$ c. oil
$\frac{1}{4}$ c. reserved mandarin orange liquid
Chopped and drained mandarin oranges
3 eggs

Glaze:
1 tbsp water
1 tbsp. Grand Mariner or other orange flavored liqueur

Heat oven to 350 degrees and flour 12-cup bundt pan. In small bowl, blend small clear packet of filling mix and $\frac{1}{3}$ cup water until smooth. Stir in remaining filling ingredients, mix well. Set aside while preparing cake batter. In large bowl, combine large clear packet of cake mix and remaining cake ingredients except orange at low speed until moistened; beat 2 minutes at medium speed. Stir in oranges; mixing well. Pour half of the batter, about 2 cups into prepared bundt pan; spread evenly. Spoon prepared filling evenly in narrow ring over center of cake batter. Filling should not touch sides of pan. Spoon remaining cake batter over filling. Carefully spread batter to edges.

Bake at 350 degrees for 40 to 50 minutes until toothpick inserted 1 inch comes out clean or top springs back when lightly touched. Cool upright in pan for 45 minutes; invert onto serving plate. Cool completely.

In small bowl, blend glaze mix. Water, and orange liqueur until smooth. If thinner glaze is desired, stir in additional water, few drops at a time. Spoon over top of cake, allowing some to fund down sides. Garnish as desired. Store loosely covered. Makes 16 servings.

ELSIE'S APRICOT CAKE

2 c. all-purpose flour
2 c. sugar
2 tsp. baking soda
½ tsp. salt
1-½ tsp. cinnamon

4 eggs
¾ c. chopped pecans
1-¼ c. cooking oil (I use 1 cup)
7 oz. jar apricot baby food

Sift dry ingredients together and set aside. Beat eggs until thick, add sugar and beat. Add dry ingredients, add baby food last. Bake in tube pan in 350 degree oven for 1 hour or a little longer. Test with toothpick. This cake stays good several days and is very good.

ELSIE'S HOLIDAY ORANGE SPONGE CAKE

1-½ c. plain flour   1-½ tsp. baking soda
¼ salt   6 eggs separated
1 c. sugar
1 tbsp. orange peel grated (I use more)
1 c. orange juice, fresh juice of 2 to 3 oranges
1 tsp. cream of tartar (put cream of tartar in egg whites)

Sift together flour, baking soda, salt in a large mixing bowl. Beat egg yolks until light. Gradually add sugar, beat until light and thick in color (about 5 minutes). Stir in orange juice and grated peel. Blend in dry ingredients alternately with the juice. Beat egg whites with the cream of tarter until stiff but not dry. Fold into batter. Pour into ten inch round cake pan. Bake in 325 degree over 50 to 60 minutes. I always test my cakes with a toothpick. Let cool before removing from pan.

Use glaze on this with powdered sugar and orange juice. Pour over the top, put in oven on broil until the glaze begins to bubble. Watch closely.

SHEILA MCCOY'S
STRAWBERRY-ANGEL FOOD CAKE

Cream filling, mix together:
8 oz. cream cheese   ⅓ c. lemon juice
1 can Eagle Brand milk   1 tsp. almond extract

Cut 1 angel food cake in half. Turn top ½ down and make a trench in center of both pieces. Fill the trench with cream filling and 2 cups chopped strawberries. Put cake back together and frost with Cool Whip.

AUNT ELOISE'S SIMPLE SOUR CREAM CAKE

1 box Duncan Hines Golden Butter Cake mix
¾ c. oil   2 tsp. vanilla
½ pint sour cream   4 eggs
½ c. sugar

In a large mixing bowl place cake mix and combine: sour cream, sugar, oil, and vanilla. Add eggs one at a time, beating after each. Mixture will be thick. Pour into greased and floured tube pan and bake at 350 degrees for 1 hour.

CHOCOLATE COCONUT PIE

4 oz. pkg. German chocolate (semi-sweet block)
3 eggs slightly beaten   ½ c. sugar
¼ c. butter   1 can evaporated milk
1-⅓ c. coconut   1 unbaked 9" pie shell

Melt chocolate and butter over low heat in a medium saucepan. Add milk, eggs, coconut, and sugar until blended. Pour into shell and bake at 400 degrees for 30 minutes. Serve warm or chilled but store in refrigerator. Top with whipped cream if desired.

CHOCOLATE PECAN BARS

Cream 1 cup butter and ⅓ cup firmly packed brown sugar, add 2 cups unsifted flour and beat until crumbly. Press evenly into bottom of 13"x9" pan. Bake at 350 degrees for 20 minutes. Melt 3 tablespoons butter and 4 oz. block chocolate over low heat. Combine 3 slightly beaten eggs, 1 cup light corn syrup, ⅓ cup light brown sugar, 1 teaspoon vanilla and chocolate mixture; mix well. Stir in 1 cup chopped pecans and 1 cup coconut. Pour over hot crust. Bake 35 to 40 minutes longer. Cool. Cut into squares.

PETE ROSE'S FAVORITE GERMAN CHOCOLATE CAKE

4 oz. pkg. German sweet chocolate
½ c. boiling water
2 c. sugar
1 tsp. vanilla
2-¼ c. sifted cake flour
1 c. buttermilk

1 c. butter or margarine
4 egg yolks
1 tsp. baking soda
½ tsp. salt
4 egg whites, stiffly beaten

Preheat oven to 350 degrees. Grease 3–9" layer pans. Melt chocolate in water. Cool. Cream butter and sugar until fluffy, add yolks one at a time, beating well. Blend in vanilla and chocolate. Sift flour with baking soda, and salt, add alternately with buttermilk to chocolate mixture, beating after each addition until smooth. Fold in whites. Pour into 3–9" layer pans and bake at 350 degrees for 30 to 35 minutes. Cool and frost tops only.

GERMAN CHOCOLATE ICING

Combine 1 cup evaporated milk, 1 cup sugar, 3 slightly beaten egg yolks, ½ cup butter, and 1 tsp. vanilla in a saucepan and cook over medium heat stirring constantly until thick, 10 to 12 minutes. Add 1-⅓ cups coconut and 1 cup chopped pecans. Spread on all three tops of cake.

CHOCOLATE FRUIT DROPS

1-¼ c. margarine
1-½ c. sugar
2-½ c. flour
8-¼ oz. can crushed pineapple, drained
1 tsp. vanilla

⅓ c. cocoa
1 tsp. baking powder
½ c. chopped nuts

1 egg

Cream margarine and sugar until fluffy, add egg and vanilla. Beat well. Combine dry ingredients and mix well. Stir in pineapple and nuts. Drop rounded teaspoons full onto greased cookie sheet and bake at 375 degrees for 12 minutes.

NO BAKE COOKIE

Oatmeal or Rice Krispies
2 c. sugar
Dash of salt
¼ c. of cocoa
¼ c. peanut butter

1 stick butter
½ c. milk
1 tsp. vanilla

Boil 1 minute, remove from heat, add 3-½ cups oats, OR cereal. Stir in ¼ cup peanut butter, roll into cookies. Cool.

YUM YUM COOKIES

Dedicated to: Kevin Todd
Melt 1 stick butter, 1 box Duncan Hines yellow cake mix, 1 egg. Mix together and beat 1 minute. Spread evenly on a sheet pan.

Mix 8 oz. package cream cheese, 2 eggs, 1 box confectioners sugar less 2 tablespoons. Pour over top. Bake at 350 degrees for 30 minutes. Cool for 1 hour and sprinkle with sugar.

THELMA OSBORNE'S ORANGE SLICE CAKE

1 lb. orange slices, chopped (orange slice candy)
8 oz. dates, chopped   2 c. pecans, chopped
1 can coconut

Flour those ingredients with ½ c. flour. Cream 1 c. butter or margarine and 2 c. sugar. Add 4 eggs, one at a time, beating well after adding each egg. Add 3 c. all-purpose flour, ½ tsp. salt, 1 tsp. vanilla, beat well. Add 1 c. buttermilk and beat well. Pour creamed mixture over flour mixture and stir until mixed. Pour into well-greased and floured tube pan. Bake at 300 degrees for 1 hour and 50 minutes; lower temperature to 275 degrees for the last 10 minutes. Remove cake from oven, leave in pan and loosen edges around outside and stem of pan.

Glaze:
2 c. confectioner's sugar dissolved in ½ c. orange juice. Pour over warm cake and cool in pan.

ELLEN'S COMPANY CHEESECAKE

1 c. sugar   1-¼ c. graham cracker crumbs
2 tbsp. sugar   2 tsp. lemon peel, grated
¼ c. butter, melted   ¼ tsp. vanilla
2 pkgs. (8 oz.) cream cheese and 1 (3 oz.) pkg.
1 c. sour cream   3 eggs

Heat oven to 350 degrees. Stir graham cracker crumbs and 2 tbsp. sugar together, mix with butter. Press into bottom of a spring form pan. Bake 10 minutes. Cool. Reduce oven heat to 300 degrees. Beat cream cheese in a large bowl, add 1 c. sugar, beat until fluffy. Add lemon peel and vanilla. Beat in eggs one at a time. Pour over crumb crust and bake for 1 hour or until center of cake is firm. Cool at room temperature for 1 hour and spread sour cream over top. Chill at least 3 hours and then loosen edges from pan with a spatula.

TRIFLE DELIGHT

1 c. heavy cream
¼ c. sugar
¾ c. apricot purée
Sliced fresh apricots
½ c. cream sherry or rum
3-¾ c. vanilla custard

3–9" round layer pound cakes
1-½ c. strawberry preserves
¼ tsp. vanilla
2 c. mandarin oranges, drained
Fresh strawberries

#1 Cut cakes in half creating 2 layers. Spread preserves on 2 cakes and apricot purée on third. Sandwich cakes together.

#2 Cut cakes into ¼" strips.

#3 Start layering to create a trifle. Line the bottom of a trifle bowl with strips from one cake. Pour rum or sherry over layer. Cover with mandarin oranges and with 1-¼ cups custard.

#4 Continue the layers without the liquor until 3 layers of each item is created.

#5 Cover and chill for 2 hours.

#6 Before serving, whip heavy cream, sugar, and vanilla until stiff. Top trifle with whipped cream.

#7 Garnish with apricots and berries and serve!

DEVILED PEANUT BUTTER & MARSHMALLOW BARS

1 box Duncan Hines devils food cake mix
1 stick butter or margarine
1 jar marshmallow cream, 7 oz. size
¾ c. peanut butter

Cream together. Place all ingredients in an ungreased 13"x9"x2" pan. Bake at 350 degrees for 20 minutes. Cool and cut into squares.

SWEDISH NUT CAKE

2 c. sugar   2 c. flour
1 can crushed pineapple with juice
2 eggs, beaten   2 tsp. baking soda
1 tsp. vanilla   ½ c. chopped nuts

Beat eggs and mix with pineapple and sugar. Add flour, baking soda, and vanilla, mixing well. Add nuts if you desire. Cake should be divided into 2 greased and floured loaf pans and baked at 325 degrees for 30 or 40 minutes until done.*

Icing:
1 pkg. (8 oz.) cream cheese   1 tbsp. vanilla
1 stick margarine   ½ c. chopped nuts
1-¾ c. confectioner's sugar

Combine all ingredients and spread on cake.

*Insert toothpick to test doneness. If it comes out clean, cake is done.

JOAN'S BIRTHDAY PARTY COOKIES

1 c. sugar
½ c. butter, softened
1 tsp. vanilla
1-½ c. all-purpose flour
¾ tsp. salt

⅓ c. nonpareils
¼ c. shortening
2 eggs
1 tsp. baking powder

Combine sugar, butter, shortening, vanilla, and eggs; beat well. Combine flour, salt and baking powder together. Add to sugar mixture and mix well. Stir in candy sprinkles (nonpareils). Cover with plastic wrap and store in refrigerator overnight.

When ready to bake, heat oven to 400 degrees. Turn cookie mixture onto a floured surface. Divide dough into 3 parts. Roll out dough and cut into desired shapes. Place on ungreased cookie sheet, 1 inch apart; and bake for 5 to 7 minutes. Remove from pan and let cool. Then ice.

Icing:

¾ c. butter, softened
2 c. confectioners sugar
2 to 3 drops food coloring of your choice

1 tsp. vanilla
1 egg

Cream together butter, confectioner's sugar, vanilla, egg, and food coloring until smooth and fluffy. Spread on cookies. Please refrigerate the iced cookies.

FRESH FRUIT PIE

Filling:
In a saucepan mix ½ cup sugar and 3 tablespoons cornstarch. Gradually stir in 1-½ cups orange juice. Stir constantly and bring to a boil over medium heat. Boil 1 minute. Remove from heat, stir in ¼ cup lemon juice and 1 teaspoon grated lemon or orange rind. Cool completely. Fold in 6 cups of assorted fruit cut up and drained.

Crust:
Stir in ¼ cup margarine, ¼ cup sugar, and 1 egg yolk. Mix 1 cup flour until crumbly. Press into a 9" pie plate and bake at 400 degrees for 8 minutes. Cool completely.

Fold in filling into crust and chill overnight or 12 hours.

*I suggest the following fruits: fresh peaches, diced; kiwi fruits, sliced; strawberries, halved; blueberries; bananas, sliced; applies, diced.

APPLE NUT COFFEE CAKE

Cake:

2 c. flour (all-purpose)	1 tsp. vanilla
1 c. sugar	1 tsp. baking soda
1 (8 oz.) carton sour cream	¼ tsp. salt
½ c. butter	2 eggs
2 c. peeled chopped apples (yellow)	

Topping:

½ c. chopped nuts	1 tsp. cinnamon
2 tbsp. butter	½ c. firmly packed brown sugar

Heat oven to 350 degrees. Combine all cake ingredients in a large bowl except apples. Beat at medium speed scraping bowl often. Fold in apples. Spread batter into well-greased 13"x9" pan. In a small bowl, combine topping ingredients. Sprinkle over batter. Bake at 350 degrees for 30 to 40 minutes or until topping is dark cinnamon brown.

CHOCOLATE WALNUT PIE

1 unbaked 9" pastry shell
2 eggs
1 c. chopped walnuts
½ tsp. vanilla

1 stick butter or margarine
¾ c. white sugar
1 c. chocolate chips

Melt butter and cool; beat eggs into butter. Add the rest of the ingredients, pour into pie shell. Bake at 350 degrees for 30 minutes.

PASTRY SHELL FOR PIES

2 c. plain flour
5 tbsp. ice water

1 c. shortening or 1 stick butter
½ tsp salt

Beat shortening and water together. Mix with flour and salt. Roll out dough into pie crust.

AUNT ELOISE'S REFRIGERATOR CAKE

1 devils food cake prepared by box directions and baked in 3 layer round pans. Cool.

Icing:
1 (12 oz.) container Cool Whip
1 c. sugar   1 (8 oz.) carton sour cream
½ c. coconut (optional)

Stir all ingredients together and ice cooled cake. Refrigerate until ready for serving. Store in refrigerator.

CHRISTMAS ROCK COOKIES

1 c. margarine
1-½ c. sugar
1 tsp. cinnamon
3 eggs
1 tsp. baking soda
2 tbsp. hot water
1 lb. (2 boxes) dates, chopped (Dromedary)

1 lb. box chopped pecans
1 box white raisins
1 tsp. cloves
1 c. chopped candied cherries
1 pinch salt
3 c. plain flour

Cut fruit into small pieces, mix well in flour. Mix sugar, margarine, cinnamon, eggs, cloves, salt, and water. Pour over floured mixture and mix well with hands. Drop by small spoonfuls onto a well greased cookie sheet and bake at 350 degrees for 8 to 10 minutes.

ORANGE BROWNIES

1 pkg. Pillsbury Plus butter recipe cake mix
⅓ c. butter, softened   1 egg
1 c. rolled oats

Heat oven to 350 degrees. Grease 13 x 9 pan. In large bowl, combine the above ingredients until crumbly, reserve 1 cup for filling. Press crumbly mixture in pan.

Filling:

6 oz. bag chocolate chips
1 c. sugar
2 eggs

1 c. chopped pecans
2 tsp. grated orange peel
¼ c. orange juice

CREPES

1-¼ c. flour
2 tbsp. sugar
Pinch of salt
3 eggs

1-½ c. milk
2 tbsp. butter, melted
1 tsp. lemon extract

Blend or mix all ingredients well. Top with bananas in syrup or cooked apples in sauce (1 tbsp. butter, ½ c. sugar, ½ c. water. Cook over medium heat for 15 minutes.) Top with sugared berries or jams.

FROZEN LEMON CREAM PIE

1 (9-inch) graham cracker crust
¼ c. lemon juice
1 c. (½ pint) whipping cream, whipped
½ c. plus 2 tbsp. sugar
3 eggs, separated

In large bowl, beat egg yolks and ½ c. sugar until light, add lemon juice. In small bowl, beat egg whites to soft peaks, gradually add sugar. Beat to stiff peaks. Fold egg whites into lemon juice mixture, gradually fold in whipped cream. Spoon into crust. Freeze 3 hours or until firm. Serve with raspberry sauce.

Raspberry Sauce:
Reserve ⅔ cup syrup from 10 ounce package thawed frozen red raspberries. In small saucepan, combine syrup, ¼ cup red currant jelly and 1 tablespoon cornstarch. Cook and stir until slightly thickened and clear. Cool. Add raspberries.

ANITA WILLOUGHBY'S PUMPKIN CAKE

2 c. flour, self-rising
2 tsp. cinnamon
2 tsp. baking soda

2 c. sugar
Dash of nutmeg

Sift all the above together.

Beat together:
4 eggs
2 c. pumpkin (small can)

1 c. oil
1 tsp. vanilla

Mix and stir this into dry ingredients. Bake at 350 degrees for 50 minutes.

Icing:
1 stick butter, softened
1 box confectioner's sugar

1 (8 oz.) pkg. cream cheese
1 tsp. vanilla

Mix together and spread on cake.

FRIED CREAM

1 qt. heavy cream
8 egg yolks
2 tsp. vanilla

½ lb. sugar
4 oz. flour

Bring cream to a boil; mix sugar flour, and egg yolks into boiling milk. Cook stirring constantly until stiff. Pour into flat pan and let cool. Cut into squares roll in flour and beaten egg and flour again (coconut optional). Fry in Crisco on medium high heat until it floats. Dust with confectioner's sugar.

WHITE FRUIT CAKE

5 c. plain flour
6 large eggs
1 lb. pineapple, crystallized
15 oz. box golden raisins
2 tsp. salt

3 c. sugar
3 sticks margarine, melted
1 lb. cherries, crystallized
2 qt. pecans
2 tsp. baking powder

1 tsp. each of lemon and white vanilla extract
¾ c. warm water

How to put it together:
Separate egg whites and whip to stiff stand. Add to yolks in large mixing bowl, whip yolks slowly adding sugar and beat to custard consistency.

Begin adding flour and melted margarine as needed to keep mix from getting too stiff. Add warm water as needed to keep from getting too stiff. Roast pecans before adding to cake. Add pecans whole, no need to chop. Switch to hand mix to add fruit and nuts. Makes about 8 lbs. of mix. It is better to divide and bake in two funnel pans. Loaf pans will do. Grease bottom and sides of pans. Cut wax paper to fit bottom of pans. Divide batter as desired for side of cakes and bake in preheated oven at 250 degrees for 2-½ hours if the oven thermostat is true. Different ovens and atmospheric pressure will cause this to vary. **Note:** Reserve 4 cherries and 8 pecan halves for top of fruitcake. After cake has baked 30 minutes place them on top of batter.

EDE STUMP'S CREAM-CICLE CAKE

One box orange supreme cake mix (a yellow cake mix will work)

Bake cake according to directions, except add milk instead of water and add 1 tsp. orange extract. Use 9" cake pans. Bake at 350 degrees for 30 to 35 minutes. Let care cool and cut into four layers.

Icing:
Beat 2–8 oz. cream cheese and 2 c. powdered sugar until smooth. Add 16 oz. Cool Whip, divide half of icing to put on each layer. Then add 1 tsp. orange extract, 4 drops yellow, and 2 drops red food coloring into icing for top and sides of cake. Add mandarin oranges on top and sides of cake. ENJOY!

GAIL ESTEP'S DREAM-CICLE CAKE

1 box cake mix (yellow or white)
1 box orange jello

Frosting:

Cool Whip (12 oz.)	2 c. sour cream
½ c. powdered sugar	½ tsp. orange zest

Butter 2 round cake pans. Prepare cake as directed adding ½ box jello to batter. Chill. Bake cake 30 minutes. Slice each layer to make 4 thin layers. Add remaining jello to frosting and zest. Top with mandarin oranges.

HARD CANDY

3-¾ c. sugar   1 c. water
1-½ c. Karo syrup   1 tsp. candy oil (any flavor)
Powdered sugar to amount

Bring sugar, water, syrup to a boil in large saucepan. Stir once after hard boil, continue for 10 minutes or until mixture forms strings standing in cold water. Remove from heat. Let boiling cease and add candy oil. Pour onto greased cookie sheets, cool for 2 or 3 hours. Take a hammer or meat tenderizer and crack into small pieces. Roll into powdered sugar. Store refrigerated. Makes about 5 dozen 1 inch pieces.

"$250.00 COOKIES"

Recipe may be halved.

2 c. butter   4 c. flour
2 tsp. baking soda   2 c. sugar
5 c. blended oatmeal   24 oz. chocolate chips
2 c. brown sugar   1 tsp. salt
8 oz. Hershey Bar, grated   4 eggs
2 tsp. baking powder   2 tsp. vanilla
3 c. chopped nuts (your choice)

Measure oats in a blender. Blend to a fine powder. Cream butter with sugars; add eggs, vanilla; mix with flour, salt, oats baking powder, and baking soda. Add chocolate chips, Hershey Bar, and nuts. Roll into balls and place 2 inches apart on cookie sheet. Bake 10 minutes at 375 degrees. Makes 112 cookies.

DEBBIE'S BROWNIES

1 c. sugar
4 eggs
1 stick margarine, softened

1 c. flour, self-rising
16 oz. can Hershey's syrup

Combine all ingredients and mix well. Pour into 13" x 9" baking pan sprayed with Pam. Bake at 350 degrees in preheated oven for 30 to 40 minutes or until done. While brownies are baking prepare topping.

Topping:

1 stick margarine
¼ c. canned cream

¾ c. sugar
½ c. chocolate chips

In small saucepan combine margarine, sugar, and cream. Bring to a boil over medium heat. Hard boil for 1 minute. Add chocolate chips and stir until melted. Can add nuts to topping if desired. Pour over hot brownies. Let cool.

JUDY'S PUMPKIN CAKE

2 c. flour, self-rising
2 tsp. cinnamon
2 tsp. baking soda
1 tsp. salt*

2 c. sugar
Dash of nutmeg
1 tsp. baking powder*

Sift all the above ingredients together. *Omit if using self-rising flour.

Beat together:
4 eggs
2 c. pumpkin, small can

1 c. oil
1 tsp. vanilla

Mix and stir into dry ingredients. Bake at 350 degrees for 50 minutes.

Icing:

1 stick butter, softened
1 box confectioner's sugar

8 oz. pkg. cream cheese
1 tsp. vanilla

Mix together and spread on cooled cake.

APPLE STACK CAKE

Cream 1 c. shortening, 1 c. sugar and 1 c. molasses. Add 3 eggs with 1 c. buttermilk. Sift 4 c. plain flour 1-½ tsp. salt, 1 tsp. ginger, and 1 tsp. cinnamon. Mix dry ingredients with shortening/molasses combination. Bake 9 thin layers at 400 degrees for 15 minutes. Spread Apple Butter* between layers and on the top.

* You can use applesauce instead of apple butter to make this cake lighter.

DADDY'S CHOCOLATE MOUSSE

Cook in double boiler on medium to medium-high heat.

To 2 qt. milk add 4 egg yolks (beaten), and 3 tbsp. cornstarch, whisk. Pour into warm milk, keep whisk moving, add 2 cups sugar. Cook until thickened and add 4 squares of semi-sweet chocolate stirring constantly, adding vanilla. Allow to cool and add whipped egg whites, chill overnight or 4 to 6 hours.

PEACHES 'N CREAM PIE

1 c. sugar
8 oz. pkg. cream cheese, room temperature
8 oz. container, whipped topping, room temperature
3 to 4 large fresh peaches, peeled, pitted
1 graham cracker pie shell

Combine sugar and cream cheese in bowl. Cream with hand mixer on high speed. Stir in whipped topping; mix on low speed until blended. Cut peaches in bite-size pieces. Layer peaches in bottom of crust. Pour cream mixture on top of peaches, spread evenly to cover. Cover pie with lid. Refrigerate overnight. The pie may be frozen; thaw before serving.

OATMEAL PIE

¾ c. sugar
¾ c. syrup
2 eggs

¾ c. oatmeal
1 stick butter, melted
Pie crust

Mix ingredients together and pour into pie crust and bake at 325 degrees for 1 hour. Options: May add, chocolate chips, coconut, pecans, and/or raisins.

ALEX'S FUDGY STYLE BROWNIES

½ c. butter or margarine
1 c. sugar
1 tsp. vanilla
¾ cup all-purpose flour + 1 c. self-rising flour
½ tsp. baking powder

6 tbsp. cocoa
1 egg
½ c. nuts, chopped
¼ tsp. salt

Mix all ingredients in a bowl and press into a 9 x 12 inch greased baking pan and bake for 30 to 35 minutes at 350 degrees.

AUSTIN'S FAVORITE REESE CUP CANDY

2-½ sticks margarine
2 c. graham cracker crumbs
12 oz. pkg. chocolate bits (semi-sweet or milk chocolate)
¼ rectangle paraffin (tray)

1 pint jar creamy peanut butter
1-½ lbs. (6 c.) confectioner's sugar

Melt margarine; add peanut butter, mix well. Add crumbs and sugar and continue to stir. If mixture becomes too thick, add more margarine and peanut butter. Spread in a rimmed cookie sheet. Melt chocolate and paraffin in a double-boiler. Spread over the crumb peanut mixture. Let candy set 15 to 20 minutes, then cut into squares.

BENITA'S BOURBON BALLS

Soften 3 sticks of butter, add 2 lbs. confectioner's sugar, 2 tbsp. vanilla, and refrigerate for 1 hour. Set out of refrigerator for 10 minutes, then add ½ c. bourbon, knead (I recommend wearing disposable kitchen gloves). Options: Stir in 1 c. finely chopped nuts or top each bourbon ball with a pecan half.

Melt 1 bag chocolate chips (16 oz.); add ½ block paraffin wax. Roll above mixture into balls and dip into melted chocolate.

PATRICK AUTRY'S DIRT PUDDING
He stomped them cookies himself!

1 bag Oreo cookies   12 oz. Cool Whip
½ stick butter
2 regular size vanilla instant pudding
8 oz. cream cheese   3 c. milk
1 c. powdered sugar

Roll out cookies, put in a 9 x 13-inch pan. Mix all ingredients. Pour over crushed cookies, sprinkle ½ c. cookies on top. Chill. Garnish with gummie worms.

FROZEN PINACHERRY PIE

1 can pineapple tidbits, drained
1 can cherry pie filling
1 container Cool Whip
1 can Eagle Brand condensed milk

Stir ingredients until smooth. Pour into ready-made graham pie crust and freeze.

STRAWBERRY YUM-YUM

1 stick margarine
2 pkgs. Dream Whip
1 c. sugar
2 c. strawberries

2 c. graham cracker crumbs
1–8 oz. cream cheese
1 c. cold milk

Melt margarine and mix with graham cracker crumbs. Place half of this mixture in the bottom of a dish. Whip the 2 pkgs. of Dream Whip as directed and add to cream cheese, sugar, and cold milk. Pour ½ on crumbs, spread sliced strawberries in a layer using the mixture between layers. Final layer should be cream cheese mixture and sprinkled with graham cracker crumbs. Chill for 3 hours.

ALEX'S COFFEE CAKE

¼ c. salad oil
½ milk
¾ sugar
½ tsp. salt

1 beaten egg
1-½ c. sifted all-purpose flour
2 tsp. baking powder
Spicy Topping

Combine salad oil, egg, and milk. Sift together dry ingredients; add to milk mixture; mix well. Pour into greased 9" x 9" x 2" pan. Sprinkle with Spicy Topping. Bake at 375 degrees about 25 minutes.

Spicy Topping:
Combine ¼ c. brown sugar, 1 tbsp. all-purpose flour, 1 tsp. ground cinnamon, 1 tbsp. melted butter, and ½ c. broken nuts.

BENITA'S FUDGE CANDY

3 c. sugar   ⅔ c. cream
1-½ stick butter
1 pkg. (12 oz.) chocolate chips or 6 oz. cocoa
1-½ c. marshmallow cream   ½ c. nuts
½ tsp. vanilla

Combine sugar, milk, and butter. Bring to boil over medium heat stirring constantly; cook for 5 minutes or until balls form in cold water. Add other ingredients and stir. Refrigerate until set; about 1–2 hours.

PUPPY CHOW

12 oz. bag butterscotch chips
2 tbsp. peanut butter
#2 size can chow mein noodles

Melt ingredients in a double boiler. Pour over noodles mixture and mix with hands then place onto greased cookie sheet until dry. Break into pieces.

FRIENDSHIP CAKE

1ˢᵗ Day: 2-½ c. sugar   1-½ c. starter juice
1 can 29 oz. peaches, chopped

Mix together with juice and heavy syrup, chop peaches with plastic knife. Stir everyday with wooden spoon.

10ᵗʰ Day: 2 c. sugar   1 can (20 oz.) pina, crushed

Stir.

20ᵗʰ Day: 2 c. sugar   2 jars
10 oz. maraschino cherries, chopped in juice

Stir.

Keep stored room temperature in plastic or class container, 1 gallon or larger. Don't close lid tight.

30ᵗʰ Day: Drain fruit, keep juice, place in jars to give as starter. Must be used in 3 to 5 days.

Makes 3 Bundt Cakes
Divide fruit into 3 parts. For each cake add:
1 box Duncan Hines Yellow cake mix
1 pkg. (3-½ oz.) vanilla instant pudding
⅔ c. oil   4 eggs
1 c. coconut   1 c. nuts

Mix first 4 ingredients together with wooden spoon, 7-½ parts of the fruit add coconut. Bake in a 300 degree oven for 1 hour or until done. Makes 3 Bundt Cakes.

BARBARA'S BUTTERSCOTCH PIE

$^1/_3$ c. white sugar
1 c. firmly packed brown sugar
1 can evaporated milk
3 egg yolks, set aside egg whites
4 tbsp. plain flour
1 pat butter

Mix sugar and flour in sauce pan, add milk and eggs, cook until thick over medium heat stirring constantly. Add 1 pat butter, stir until smooth. Pour thick pudding mixture into a baked, frozen pie shell (any brand).

MERINGUE

Beat 3 egg whites until stiff. Add $^1/_3$ c. sugar and 1 tsp. vanilla. Beat until smooth. Spread on top of pie and broil meringue.

This pie recipe can be used for any cream pie. Substitute brown sugar for white and add either cocoa for chocolate; add lemon juice for lemon; add peanut butter to brown sugar recipe; add vanilla for a custard pie.

– 5 –

MEATS

NOTES

BACONY CHICKEN BREASTS

1 can (16 oz.) white new potatoes, drained
1 can (6 oz) sliced mushrooms, drained
Salt   4 slices bacon, cut in quarters
2 tbsp. butter or margarine   1 tbsp. salad oil
4 chicken cutlets, about 2 lbs.

Preheat broiler. Slice potatoes ½ inch thick. Pat dry with paper towel. Arrange in bottom of 13" x 9" broiler pan. Cover with mushrooms. Sprinkle lightly with salt. Top with bacon slices. Broil 10 minutes, turning occasionally. Meanwhile, in large heavy skillet, melt butter with oil over medium-high heat. Lightly sprinkle both sides of chicken breasts with salt. Sauté 2 to 3 minutes per side. Transfer to serving dish. Top with broiled potatoes, mushrooms, and bacon. Makes 4 servings, 335 calories each.

MOIST AND CRISPY ONION CHICKEN

1 envelope Lipton Onion Recipe Soup Mix
¾ c. fine dry bread crumbs
1 (2-½ to 3-¼ lb.) broiler-fryer chicken, cut in parts
½ c. Hellman's Real Mayonnaise

Place onion soup and bread crumbs in large plastic food bag and shake to blend. Brush chicken on all sides with mayonnaise. Place one piece of chicken in bag at a time, close bag tightly and shake until coated. Place chicken on rack in broiler pan. Bake in 400 degree oven for 40 to 45 minutes or until golden brown and tender. Serves 4.

SOUPIER SLOPPY JOE

¼ lb. ground beef   ½ c. water
1 envelope Lipton Tomato Cup-a-Soup

In small skillet, brown ground beef, drain. Stir in Cup-a-Soup blended with water. Simmer, stirring occasionally, 5 minutes. Serve, if desired, on toasted hamburger roll. Makes 1 serving.

MEAT BALLS AND RED SAUCE

1 lb. ground round   2 cloves minced garlic
2 eggs   1-½ fresh bread crumbs

Mix all ingredients together and roll into balls. Fry meatballs in 1" olive oil. Remove from pan and drain. Pour remaining oil from skillet.

Add:
2 c. tomato sauce   1 tsp. oregano
2 tsp. basil

Place meatballs back in skillet in above ingredients. Simmer until meatballs are warm. Serve over cooked and drained rotini noodles. Sprinkle with Parmesan cheese.

FETTUCCINI CRAB MEAT

1 box fettuccini noodles, cooked and drained
In large sauce pot; melt 1 stick butter and 2 cloves minced garlic. Pour cooked noodles into garlic butter.

Add:
1-½ c. half and half   1 lb. steamed fresh crab meat
1 c. fresh grated Parmesan cheese

Sprinkle with parsley, salt, and pepper. Stir together, serve hot.

LASAGNA

Beef Mixture:
Brown 1 lb. ground round, drain well, add one chopped onion, 1 c. chopped mushrooms, 1 c. chopped tomato, 2 cloves garlic minced, 1 tbsp. Spaghetti sauce seasoning, 1 tsp. oregano, 1 tsp. basil, 1 large can tomato sauce, 1 small can tomato paste, 1 green pepper, chopped.

Cheeses:

1 c. cottage cheese	2 c. grated mozzarella cheese
1 c. grated Parmesan cheese	1 c. grated Swiss

1 pkg. lasagna noodles, cooked and drained

Start with lasagna noodles and layer each item one at a time (example: lasagna noodles, beef mixture, and cheeses). Top with tomato ketchup, grated Parmesan and basil. Bake at 350 degrees for 1 hour.

SPAGHETTI

Brown 1 lb. ground round and drain

Add:

1 chopped onion	2 cloves garlic, minced
1 c. chopped mushrooms	1 green pepper, chopped
1 red pepper, chopped	1 tsp. basil
2 tbsp. oregano	1 tbsp. spaghetti sauce seasoning
1 c. water	1 small can tomato paste
1 large can tomato sauce	

Simmer all ingredients on low heat for 2 hours. Serve over one pound of spaghetti noodles, cooked and drained.

CINDY'S LASAGNA

1 lb. Italian sausage
1 tbsp. basil leaves
3 c. cottage cheese
2 tbsp. parsley, chopped
1-½ tsp oregano
1 (12 oz.) can tomato paste
½ tsp. pepper
1 lb. Mozzarella cheese, grated or sliced

10 oz. lasagna noodles
2 cloves garlic, minced
½ c. grated Romano cheese
2 eggs, well beaten
2 c. tomatoes, crushed
1 tsp. salt

Cook lasagna noodles in boiling water for 20 minutes, drain, rinse, and set aside. Brown sausage and garlic slowly; pour off excess grease and add basil, salt, oregano, tomatoes, and tomato paste. Simmer 30 minutes uncovered. In a bowl, mix cottage cheese, Romano cheese, parsley flakes, eggs, sale, and pepper. In a 13" x 9" x 2-½" baking dish, place ½ the noodles, then spread ½ the cheese filling on the noodles; spread ½ the Mozzarella cheese on the cheese filling, then the meat sauce. Repeat layers and bake 30 minutes at 375 degrees. Serves 8.

SAUSAGE CHILI

1 lb. beef sausage
1 medium onion, chopped
¼ tsp. garlic powder
Cayenne pepper (optional)
1–8 oz. can tomato sauce
1 tsp. ground cumin

1 can red kidney beans
½ c. water
1 tsp. salt
1 lb. can tomatoes
2–3 tbsp. chili powder

Combine and fry sausage and onion together until sausage is lightly cooked. Add beans. Crush tomatoes and add with their juice; combine all other ingredients and add to pot. Simmer, uncovered for an hour or more. Serves 4.

DAVID'S WIMPY BURGERS

1-½ lb. ground round   1 envelope onion soup mix
3 tbsp. Worcestershire sauce

Mix together with hands. Make into patties. Grill until desired doneness. Serve on toasted buns.

ORANGE ROUGHY FISH

6 Orange Roughy fillets, washed and patted dry

Place fish flat in greased casserole dish. Layer 1 stick butter cut into pats over fish. Squeeze juice of 1 lemon over top of butter and fish. Place 1 tsp. of champagne mustard on top of each fillet. Sprinkle with tarragon; pour ¼ c. white wine over fish. Bake uncovered in 350 degree oven for 25 to 30 minutes or until fish is flaky.

CORNISH FLAMBÉ WITH CHERRIES

4 Cornish Game Hens   ½ tsp salt
¼ lb. cherries, pitted   1 tbsp. cornstarch
2 c. red wine   2 tsp. water
½ tsp. cinnamon   ½ stick butter
1 tsp. bell pepper flakes   1 c. Kirsch

Rinse Cornish hens and pat dry. Place on Spanek Roaster and set in roasting pan with 1-½ c. water in bottom. Cook hens in preheated oven at 450 degrees for 15 minutes; reduce heat to 375 degrees and roast 30 minutes longer. Place cherries in a pan with red wine, cinnamon, bell pepper flakes, and salt. Cook slowly, covered for 30 minutes. Strain sauce, reserving cherries and peppers and return to liquid on medium heat. Mix cornstarch and water. Add to sauce a little at a time. Reduce to simmer. Add butter and heat until melted. Just before serving, add reserved cherries and peppers. Heat sauce 5 minutes more. Add a glass of Kirsch and flambé. Serves 4.

AUNT KAT'S TENDERLOIN

Pork tenderloin
Soy sauce
Onion

Place tenderloin in oven and cover with soy sauce and onion. Bake at 300 degrees for 1-½ hours.

FAYE MCCOY'S SUKIYAKI

3 strips steak, sliced thin and trimmed
4 stalks celery, chopped   1 onion, chopped
1 green pepper, chopped   ½ c. soy sauce
Seasoned salt and pepper   1 bag frozen mixed vegetables
½ c. cooking oil   1 stick butter

In wok, heat oil and soy sauce. Stir-fry meat until tender, and add seasoned salt and pepper. In saucepan, sauté onion, pepper, and celery in butter. Cook vegetables according to package directions, drain. Add all ingredients to wok and simmer for 20 minutes. Serve with fresh melon such as cantaloupe or honey dew, and French bread, and sliced tomatoes.

FLORENE'S BEEF ROAST

Roll a 3 pound roast in flour. Brown the roast in shortening. Put 1-½ cups water and 1 medium onion in cooker. Cook for half an hour, add 1 can of Golden Mushroom soup. Salt and pepper to taste, and cook another hour on medium heat or until tender.

CHICKEN CACCIATORE

8 boneless, skinless chicken breasts, boiled until tender

In sauce pot, cook 2 cans (12 oz.) tomato sauce, 2 tbsp. basil, 1 tsp. oregano, 1 garlic clove, minced, salt and pepper to taste, ½ c. Parmesan cheese, grated. Pour over chicken that has been placed in greased casserole dish. Bake 350 degrees for 45 minutes. Serve over hot buttered noodles or rice.

UNCLE JACKIE'S JAMBALAYA

4 small bay leaves   1 tsp. salt
¼ tsp. white pepper   ¼ tsp. red pepper
⅛ tsp. black pepper   1 tsp. dry mustard
½ tsp. ground cumin   ½ tsp. thyme
1-½ clove garlic, minced

Mix all above ingredients together and set aside.

4 tbsp butter or margarine   6 oz. smoked ham
1-½ c. smoked sausage   1-½ c. onion, chopped
1-½ celery, chopped   1 bell pepper, chopped
2 c. rice   4 c. beef broth
1 can tomatoes

Mix all above meet ingredients together and add the above seasoning ingredients and pour into large cooker. Simmer for 1 hour. Cook rice separately and serve Jambalaya over rice.

SPANISH CHICKEN AND SAUSAGE

4 chicken breasts, halved   4 chicken drumsticks
½ tsp. salt   ⅛ tsp. pepper
⅛ tsp. paprika   3 tbsp. olive oil
½ sweet sausage, cut ½" lengths
½ lb. hot sausage, cut ½" lengths
1 c. chopped onions   1 c. chopped green pepper
2 cloves garlic, minced   1 c. raw regular rice
¼ tsp. powdered saffron   2 tsp. capers
2 c. boiling chicken broth   1 c. frozen peas
10 stuffed olives

Wash chicken, dry; sprinkle with salt, pepper, and paprika. Heat olive oil in Paella Pan over medium high heat for 1 minute; add chicken, brown on all sides, about 15 minutes; reducing heat to medium after 5 minutes; remove from pan. Add sausages, onions, green peppers, garlic; sauté 2 to 3 minutes; remove pan from heat. Add rice, saffron, capers, broth; stir to blend. Arrange chicken pieces on top; bake uncovered 15 minutes at 400 degrees. Remove from oven; go around sides of pan with spoon to push rice back into the liquid; sprinkle peas, olives over top. Return to oven; bake additional 10 to 15 minutes or until liquid has been absorbed. Serve directly from Paella Pan. Serves eight.

SOUR CREAM PORK CHOPS

6 to 8 large pork chops, washed and dried.

Brown chops in large skillet.

Mix together:

½ c. water   2 tbsp. chopped onion
2 tbsp. brown sugar   2 tbsp. ketchup
1 clove garlic, minced   1 beef bullion cube

Mix the above ingredients together and pour over browned chops. Cover and simmer for 40 minutes. Remove chops and keep warm. In small bowl, combine 2 tbsp. flour and ¼ c. water. Slowly add this to mixture in skillet and cook until thickened. Stir in ½ c. sour cream. Put chops in a casserole dish and pour this sauce over chops and serve.

CHICKEN WITH SHALLOTS AND ARTICHOKE HEARTS

1 pkg. Pepperidge Farm pastry shells
6 tbsp. butter or margarine   2 tbsp. vegetable oil
3 whole chicken breasts, skinned, boned and cut into slivers
16 whole shallots   Salt and pepper
1 bay leaf   ½ c. chicken broth
1 pkg. (10 oz) frozen artichoke hearts, thawed
½ c. heavy cream
1 tbsp. butter or margarine mixed with 2 tbsp. flour

Prepare pastry shells according to package directions. In large skillet, heat butter and oil over high heat. Add chicken and cook, stirring constantly, until meat loses its pink color. Transfer to plate. Add shallots to fat in pan and cook until tender and glazed. Return chicken to pan; add salt, pepper and bay leaf. Cook over high heat until chicken is browned. Add chicken broth and artichoke hearts and cooked until tender. Just before serving, stir in heavy cream. If necessary, thicken gravy with butter-flour mixture cooking and stirring constantly. Spoon into warm pastry shells and serve. Serves 6.

SPANISH PAELLA

2 lbs. chicken   6 small lobster tails (12 oz.)
½ lb. raw shrimp in shells   ½ lb. smoked sausage links
¼ c. olive oil   ½ lb. frozen haddock (optional)
1 dz. Mussels or small clams in shells
Sofrito (subtly seasoned base sauce)
¼ c. olive oil   1 tsp. instant minced garlic
¼ c. instant minced onion
1 large tomato, peeled, finely chopped
1 medium green pepper cut in 2" x ¼"
¼ tsp powdered saffron   2 c. long grain wild rice, raw
1 tsp. salt   5 c. boiling water
½ c. defrosted frozen peas   2 lemons, cut into wedges
¼ lb. lean pork, cut in ¼ inch cubes

Wash, dry chicken, cut in 12 pieces; sprinkle with salt and pepper. Thaw lobster tails if frozen, cut along shell to remove membrane covering meat; cut through shell, slicing tails into 1" pieces. Clean shrimp leaving tails intact. Cut sausage links into 1" pieces. Partially thaw haddock, cut into 1" cubes. Arrange chicken, lobster, shrimp, sausage, haddock on large tray. Heat olive oil in Paella Pan 2 to 3 minutes over medium high heat; reduce heat to medium; quickly brown fish and meats one at a time in order given above; return to tray after browning (total time about 25 minutes) add additional 1 to 2 teaspoons olive oil if necessary.

To Make Sofrito:

Heat olive oil in Paella Pan 1 to 2 minutes over medium high heat; reduce heat to medium; add pork cubes, browning quickly; add onion, garlic, green peppers, tomato; cook briskly stirring constantly until most of the liquid evaporates and mixture thickens (total time about 10 to 12 minutes). Add rice, saffron, salt, water; bring to boil stirring constantly—about 5 minutes; remove from heat. Arrange chicken pieces on top of rice; fill in spaces with lobster, shrimp, sausage, haddock, and mussels making an attractive display; scatter peas at random over the whole. Place pan on lowest rack position of oven. Bake uncovered 30 to 35 minutes at 400 degrees or until all liquid has been absorbed by the rice. (NOTE: Rice grains should be tender but not too soft.) DO NOT stir Paella after it goes into the oven. When Paella is done, remove from the oven; drape a kitchen towel loosely over top; let rest about 5 minutes. Garnish Paella with lemon wedges, serve at tables directly from Paella Pan. Makes 6 servings.

TOMATO PORK CASSEROLE
(Double if Desired)

4 pork loins or chops	1 c. rice
1 can tomatoes, chopped	2 c. water
1 onion, sliced	Seasonings to taste

Brown pork on both sides; layer with rice, onion, and tomatoes in baking dish. Pour in water and sprinkle in seasonings. Bake at 350 degrees for 1 hour.

BAKED HAM WITH PARMESAN CRUST

3 to 4 lbs. fully cooked boneless ham

¼ c. dry bread crumbs	8-¼ oz. can pineapple chunks
¼ c. grated Parmesan cheese	½ c. light corn syrup
2 tbsp. chopped parsley	¼ c. butter or margarine
Dash salt and pepper	3 tbsp. Dijon-style mustard
2 c. green beans	¼ tsp ground allspice
¼ c. diced red pepper	

Score top of ham. Drain pineapple chunks, reserving juice, set aside. In a small bowl combine pineapple juice, corn syrup, butter, mustard, and allspice; mix well. For Parmesan crust, combine bread crumbs, cheese, parsley, salt, and pepper. Brush pineapple glaze over surface of ham. Press crumb mixture into ham. Place ham in a shallow baking pan. Bake in a 325-degree oven for 1-½ to 2 hours or until crust is golden and ham is heated through. Steam vegetables; combine with pineapple chunks. Coat with remaining glaze. Makes 4 servings plus leftovers.

CORNISH ITALIANO

2 to 3 Cornish Game Hens (halved)

⅛ tsp. pepper	1-½ tsp. sage
1 tsp. rosemary	1 tsp. salt
1 tsp. garlic powder	2 tbsp. butter
2 tbsp. olive oil	1 c. dry white wine
1 tbsp. flour	

Mix dry ingredients and rub game hens inside and out. In Dutch oven melt butter and oil and brown hens on all sides. Add wine, cover and simmer until tender (approximately 45 minutes). Remove hens to platter, cover and keep warm. Mix flour with ½ c. warm water and add to pan juices for Cornish sauce. Serve with noodles mixed with sour cream and Parmesan cheese.

BARBECUE-STYLE SIRLOIN TIP

3 to 4 lbs. sirloin tip roast
1 garlic clove, split (optional)
1 (18 oz.) bottle barbecue sauce

Rub meat surface with split garlic, if desired. To marinate, place roast in a plastic bag, set in deep bowl. Pour barbecue sauce over meat, close bag. Marinate in the refrigerator 2 to 24 hours, turning occasionally. Place roast, fat side up, in a shallow pan reserving barbecue sauce. Insert a meat thermometer in the center of meat till bulb rests in the thickest part of the meat. Roast, covered, in a 325 degree oven (30 to 35 minutes per pound for medium rare, 140 degrees). For smaller roasts, use higher minutes per pound. Remove roast from oven after 30 minutes. Add reserved sauce to the bottom of pan. Cover and return to oven. Remove roast from oven when thermometer register 135 degrees, allow to stand, covered with foil about 15 to 20 minutes before carving. Makes 4 servings plus leftovers.

GLAZED PORK TENDERLOIN

3 to 4 lbs. pork tenderloin
1 garlic clove, split
1 (10 oz.) jar currant jelly
1 tsp. shredded orange peel
2 tbsp. orange juice

2 tbsp. lemon juice
1 tbsp. butter or margarine
1-½ tsp. grated gingerroot or
¼ tsp. ground ginger
1 tsp. Dijon-style mustard

Place roast fat side up, on a rack in a shallow pan, rub split garlic over surface. Insert a meat thermometer. Roast in 325 degree oven for 1-½ hours or until thermometer registers 165 degrees. Let stand 10 minutes, allowing internal temperature to rise to 170 degrees. Meanwhile, in a small saucepan, combine currant jelly, orange peel, lemon juice, butter, gingerroot, and mustard. Heat until sauce is smooth. Baste roast with currant sauce the last ½ hour of roasting. Serve warm with pork. Makes 4 servings plus leftovers.

LEMON-HERB CHICKEN

1 pkg. Holly Farm Nuggets
2 tbsp. flour
¼ tsp. salt
Dash pepper

2 tbsp. butter or margarine
½ c. chicken broth
1 tbsp. lemon juice
¼ tsp. basil leaves, crushed

Combine flour, salt, and pepper, toss with chicken nuggets. Brown chicken on all sides in butter. Add remaining ingredients. Cover and simmer 10 minutes or until tender. Serve with rice. Serves 3.

TERIYAKI STIR-FRY

1 pkg. Holly Farm Nuggets
4 tbsp. teriyaki sauce
1 c. broccoli flowerets
Oil

1 tsp. cornstarch
⅓ c. chicken broth
¼ tsp. sugar

Combine chicken nuggets and 2 tbsp. teriyaki sauce. Stir-fry broccoli in oil for 1 minute. Remove. Stir-fry chicken in 2 tbsp. oil until brown on all sides. Combine 2 tbsp. teriyaki sauce and remaining ingredients; pour over chicken. Bring to boil, add broccoli. Cover and simmer until chicken and broccoli are tender. Serve with rice. Serves 3.

HERB-MARINATED LAMB

4 lamb leg steaks, ½ inch thick (1 to 1-½ lbs.)
⅔ c. cooking oil
½ c. chopped onion
¼ c. apple cider vinegar
¼ c. red wine
1 garlic clove, minced

1 tsp. salt
½ tsp. dried rosemary, crushed
½ dried thyme, crushed
Dash pepper
½ c. mint jelly, melted

Slash fat edges of lamb steaks in several places to keep steaks flat while broiling. To marinate, place steaks in a plastic bag; set in a deep bowl. Combine oil, onion, vinegar, wine, garlic, salt, rosemary, thyme, and pepper. Pour herb mixture over steaks; close bag. Marinate in the refrigerator for 6 hours, turning occasionally. Place steaks on an unheated rack in a broiler pan, reserving 3 tbsp. of marinade. Broil 3 inches from heat for 5 to 7 minutes more to desired doneness. Combine mint jelly and marinade; serve warm with lamb steaks. Makes 4 servings.

CRISP COD CAKES AND HERB MAYONNAISE

1-½ lbs. cod fillet
2 tsp. chopped parsley
½ c. mayonnaise
3 scallions, diced
¼ tsp. crushed fennel seeds
⅛ tsp. hot pepper sauce
3 tbsp. oil

1-½ tsp. lemon juice
Salt and pepper
2 eggs, beaten to mix
1 c. fresh bread crumbs
¼ tsp. dried thyme
½ c. flour

Put fish in a frying pan with ½" water, cover, and simmer until just done, about 10 minutes. Drain, flake fish into a bowl and let cool. Stir lemon juice, parsley, and ⅛ tsp. pepper into mayonnaise. Stir eggs, scallions, bred crumbs, fennel, thyme, hot pepper sauce, ½ tsp. salt, and ⅛ tsp. pepper into flaked fish. Shape into 8 patties. Dredge in flour. Sauté in oil over medium high heat until gold brown, about 7 minutes a side. Serve with herb mayonnaise.

SHRIMP CURRY

1 pkg. Pepperidge Farm pastry shells
3 tbsp. butter or margarine
⅓ c. chopped onion
1 tbsp. all-purpose flour
1 tsp. salt
½ tsp. minced peeled garlic
1-½ tsp. curry powder
Chutney
1 c. light cream, half and half, or milk
1-½ lbs. fresh shrimp, peeled, de-veined, and cooked
Shredded coconut

Prepare pastry shells according to package directions. In a medium saucepan heat butter until melted. Add onion and garlic and cook until soft and transparent. Stir in flour, curry powder, and salt and cook 1 to 2 minutes, stirring constantly. Remove from heat and stir in cream, beating until smooth. Cook 5 to 7 minutes longer over moderate heat, stirring constantly until thick and smooth. Stir in shrimp and cook until heated through. Spoon shrimp into warm pastry shells and serve with chutney and coconut. Makes 6 servings.

SHRIMP AND ASPARAGUS STIR-FRY

2 tbsp. vegetable oil
1 lb. asparagus, cut in 1-½ " pieces
2 red peppers, cut in 1-½ " pieces
1-½ lbs. medium shrimp, peeled and de-veined
2 tbsp. soy sauce   4 cloves garlic, minced
1-½ tsp. sesame oil   1-½ tsp. grated fresh ginger
Grated zest of 1 lemon   ¼ tsp red pepper flakes
¼ tsp. salt   2 tbsp. chopped fresh coriander
1 scallion, sliced

Heat the vegetable oil in a large frying pan or wok over medium-high heat. Add asparagus and red pepper and cook, stirring, until almost tender, about 8 minutes. Add the shrimp and soy sauce and continue to cook until the shrimp turn pink, about 3 minutes. Add the sesame oil, garlic, lemon zest, ginger, salt, and red pepper flakes. Cook until hot. 2 to 3 minutes. Serve with the scallion and coriander scattered over the top.

CUMIN MEATBALLS

16 oz. can plum tomatoes   1 onion, chopped
2 cloves garlic, minced   1-¼ tsp. ground cumin
Salt and pepper   1 tbsp. plus 1 tsp. oil
¼ tsp. red pepper flakes   1 egg, lightly beaten
1-½ lbs. ground beef   1 c. dry bread crumbs
2-½ tbsp. milk   1 bunch fresh coriander

Purée tomatoes with their liquid in a food processor. Sauté onion, garlic, ¼ tsp. cumin, and ½ tsp. salt in 1 tbsp. oil until onion is soft, 2 to 3 minutes. Add tomato purée and red pepper flakes. Simmer over low heat, partly covered, 30 minutes. In a large bowl, mix egg, beef, bread crumbs, milk, ½ tsp. pepper, ¾ tsp. salt and 1 tsp. cumin. Shape into 1" balls. Cook meatballs in 1 tsp. oil until browned all over, 10 to 15 minutes. Top each meatball with a coriander leaf, spear with a toothpick and serve with sauce.

LAMB CHOPS WITH LEMON DILL SAUCE

1 lemon
1 tsp. cornstarch
1 c. chicken stock
½ tsp. dried dill

2 egg yolks
4 lamb chops
2 tsp. oil

Squeeze 2 tbsp. of the juice from the lemon. Whisk the egg yolks and then the cornstarch. Sauté the lamb chops in the oil until browned on both sides, about 8 minutes in all. Transfer to warm platter or plates. Pour off the fat in the pan, add the chicken stock and dill and brink to a boil, scraping up any browned bits. Slowly whisk the hot stock into the lemon mixture. Pour this mixture back into the pan and cook over low heat, stirring constantly until thickened, about 2 minutes. Serve the sauce with the lamb chops.

CHICKEN PICCATA

2 whole skinned and boned chicken breasts, halved lengthwise
Dash salt and pepper   1 clove garlic, minced
¼ c. flour
¼ c. dry white wine or chicken broth
4 tbsp. butter or margarine   2 tbsp. lemon juice
1 c. fresh sliced mushrooms   2 tbsp. chopped parsley

Place chicken between 2 pieces of plastic wrap. Pound chicken to ½ inch thickness. Sprinkle chicken with salt and pepper, coat with flour. In a large skillet brown chicken in 3 tbsp. of butter over medium heat about 5 minutes or until lightly golden. Remove from skillet and keep warm. Add remaining butter to the skillet and cook the mushrooms and garlic until tender. Return chicken to pan; add wine and lemon juice. Simmer for 7 to 10 minutes, stirring occasionally, until sauce thickens. Top with parsley. Serves 4.

MOTHER'S CELESTIAL GOLD CHICKEN

4 large chicken breast, split, skinned, and deboned
Salt and pepper
Flour
2 eggs slightly beaten

⅓ c. butter
1 tsp. water
Fine bread crumbs

Filling:
2 c. finely shredded cabbage
1-½ tbsp chopped pimento
¼ c. finely chopped green onion
2 tbsp. sugar
½ stick butter

Dash allspice
½ tsp. salt

1 c. chopped, drained, rinsed bean sprouts
1 c. finely chopped water chestnuts
¼ tsp. dried basil leaves

Sauce:
1 c. whipping cream
¾ c. chicken broth
¼ c. chopped onion
1 clove minced garlic

2 tbsp. butter
2 tbsp. soy sauce
2 tbsp. flour
Chow Mein Noodles

For Filling:
Cook cabbage and green onions in butter until tender, add remaining ingredients and heat until hot, then let cool. Next cover each chicken breast with plastic wrap; flatten with meat hammer or rolling pin, until 1/8" thick, taking care not to tear chicken. Peel off plastic wrap, salt and pepper chicken. Place ¼ c. filling in center of each piece of chicken. Roll up tightly folding in the ends. Dip chicken in flour, shaking off excess. Next dip in eggs and water, which have been blended together; then in bread crumbs, coating well. Brown in butter in skillet. Arrange in greased baking dish (11-¾" x 7-½").

For Sauce:
Cook onions and garlic together until golden brown about 3 minutes. Blend in ½ c. broth, cream, and soy sauce. Pour sauce over chicken. Cover and bake 45 minutes at 350 degrees, remove cover, and bake for 15 minutes longer.

VEAL PARMIGIANA

Tomato sauce (see below) | 2 eggs beaten
1 to 1-¼ lbs. thinly sliced boneless veal
4 oz. mozzarella cheese, sliced
½ c. dry bread crumbs | Hot cooked fettuccine (optional)
½ c. grated Parmesan cheese

Tomato Sauce:
In a heavy saucepan, cook ¼ cup chopped onion and 1 minced garlic clove in 1 tbsp. cooking oil until tender. Add (28 oz.) can undrained whole tomatoes, broken up, 1 tbsp. sugar, 1 tsp. dried oregano, 1 tsp. dried basil, ¼ tsp. salt, and dash of pepper. Simmer for 30 to 40 minutes, stirring occasionally, until thickened, set aside.

Meanwhile, cut veal into 8 pieces. Combine bread crumbs and Parmesan cheese. Dip veal pieces in egg, coat with crumb mixture. Let stand about 20 minutes or until coating begins to dry. In a large skillet, brown veal in hot oil over medium heat about 8 minutes or until golden. Place veal pieces in baking dish. Spoon Tomato Sauce over and top with cheese slice. Bake in 375 degree oven for 8 to 10 minutes or until veal is tender. Makes 4 servings.

CORNISH HENS AND WALNUT-APPLE STUFFING

6 Tyson Cornish Game Hens | 3 oz. walnut pieces
Paprika, salt, pepper | 2 apples, cored, and chopped
Oil | ⅓ c. port
3 c. cooked wild rice | ½ tsp. salt
¼ c. finely chopped celery | Pepper
¼ c. finely chopped onion | 1 tbsp. parsley flakes

Wash hens and pat dry, season with salt, paprika, and pepper. Rub gently with oil. Add remaining ingredients for stuffing and toss lightly. Divide stuffing among hens and truss. Place in roasting pan and roast for 1 hour or until tender in preheated 350 degree oven. Serves 6. Serve with candied yams, broccoli with Hollandaise and slivered almonds and dill bread.

COUNTRY CORNISH HENS

3 Tyson Cornish Hens (halved)
1 tbsp. paprika
2 c. sour cream   1 tbsp. salt
¼ c. lemon juice   ½ tsp. pepper
2 tbsp. Worcestershire sauce   2 c. dry bread crumbs
2 tbsp. celery salt

In large bowl, combine sour cream, lemon juice, celery salt, paprika, salt, and pepper. Dip each Cornish half in mixture. Coat with bread crumbs. Arrange in single layer in large shallow baking pan. Bake uncovered in preheated 350 degree oven for 45 minutes or until tender. Serves 6. Serve with au gratin potatoes, green beans, and buttermilk biscuits.

BEEF STROGANOFF

1 lb. beef tenderloin, sliced into thin strips
2 c. fresh mushrooms, chopped
4 beef bullion cubes dissolved in ½ c. hot water
½ c. dry white wine   1 large onion, chopped
1 c. sour cream   2 cloves garlic, minced
1 oz. Worcestershire sauce   1 oz. A-1 steak sauce
1 bag egg noodles, cooked and drained
1 oz. Heinz 57 sauce

Sauté beef in butter and minced garlic until done. Add mushrooms, onions, bullion, wine, sour cream, steak sauces, and simmer on low heat about 20 minutes. Pour beef mixture over hot noodles and serve PRONTO! You can use ground round in place of beef tenderloin. Brown and drain well.

APRICOT CHICKEN

1 small jar apricot preserves
1 envelope Lipton's onion soup mix
3 tbsp. honey
1 small bottle French dressing
2 lbs. chicken, cut up and skinned

Stir together and pour over washed and skinned chicken. Bake at 350 degrees for 1 hour.

You can use this sauce over pork also. Orange marmalade, peach preserves, pineapple preserves can also be used in place of apricot preserves.

MUSHROOM CHICKEN

2 lbs. chicken, washed, skinned, and cut up

Mix together 1 can cream of mushroom soup, 1 cup water, 1 large onion, chopped. Pour over chicken and bake at 350 degrees for 45 minutes to 1 hour.

PEPPER CHICKEN

2 lbs. chicken, washed, skinned, and cut up
1 jar pineapple preserves   1 jar (10 oz.) Heinz 57 sauce
2 green peppers, cored, and chunked
2 red peppers, cored, and chunked
2 large onions, quartered
Squeeze butter
Honey

Mix preserves, Heinz 57 sauce, onions, and peppers together. Squeeze butter and honey over chicken. Bake at 350 degrees for 45 minutes to 1 hour.

SEASONED CHICKEN

2 lbs. chicken, washed, cut up, and skinned. Greased casserole dish, layer chicken flat into dish. Sprinkle with seasoned salt and pepper.

4 chicken bullion cubes
2 c. hot water
1 stick butter

Mix the above 3 ingredients together and pour over chicken and cover. Bake at 350 degrees for 1 hour.

JOAN'S MAPLE TERIYAKI SALMON FILLETS

$\frac{1}{3}$ c. apple juice
3 tbsp. soy sauce
2 garlic cloves, minced

$\frac{1}{3}$ c. maple syrup
2 tbsp. onion, finely chopped
4 salmon fillets—about 2 lbs.

Combine first 5 ingredients. Remove $\frac{1}{2}$ c. for basting. Marinate 1 to 3 hours. Broil or grill.

JORGE F. SARDINA'S CARNE FRIA (COLD MEAT)

2 lb. ground sirloin, beef
$\frac{1}{2}$ c. Romano cheese
2 tbsp. parsley
1 tbsp. salt
1 tbsp. oregano

2 eggs
1 c. Italian bread crumbs
$\frac{1}{2}$ tsp. pepper
$\frac{1}{4}$ c. milk
1 onion, chopped

Pour 1 cup of broth and $\frac{1}{2}$ cup of tomato sauce before cooking then put in oven. Cook at 350 degrees for 1-$\frac{1}{2}$ hours.

TORTELLINI AND CREAM SAUCE

Cook cheese tortellini per package instructions.

Sauce:
Sauté 1 small onion in 3 tbsp. butter; add ¼ lb. prosciutto cut into strips, 1 cup small baby peas, 1 cup cream, and salt and pepper to taste.

PEANUT CRUSTED CRAB CAKES

¼ c. onion, chopped
⅓ c. carrots, finely shredded
¼ c. mayonnaise
½ c. saltines, finely crushed, or cracker meal
1 tsp. Old Bay Seasoning
1 lb. fresh lump crabmeat, flaked, or three cans lump crabmeat, drained, flaked, and cleaned
⅓ c. honey roasted peanuts, finely chopped

1 tbsp. butter
1 egg
1 tbsp. yellow mustard

½ c. peanut oil

Mix ingredients together well using hands, form into patties and fry until golden brown.

CORNFLAKE CHICKEN

Roll chicken breasts in honey and dijon mustard. Sprinkle with paprika. Spray pan heavily with Pam. Place breasts in cornflake crumbs and crunched flakes. Spray chicken heavily with Pam. Bake at 325° for 1 hour and 15 minutes.

AUNT JO'S MEAT LOAF

2 lbs. ground beef
1 c. bread crumbs
½ c. milk
2 eggs

4 small onions, chopped
½ c. celery, chopped
Salt and pepper

Pour milk on crumbs, add eggs and mix; add onion, celery, salt and pepper and mix in to ground beef. Form into a loaf and bake in a slow oven for 1 hour. Add ½ sauce on top of loaf and bake 1 hour longer. Use the remaining sauce when the loaf is done.

Sauce:
¼ c. brown sugar
1 c. water
2 tsp. horseradish

1 tsp. mustard (jar)
1 tsp. Worcestershire sauce

BAKED BEEF HASH

4 c. diced leftover roast beef
¼ c. onion, finely chopped
¼ c. butter
½ c. dry red wine
6 large boiled potatoes, diced
½ c. heavy cream

2 tbsp. soy sauce
2 tbsp. parsley, chopped
1 tsp. ground marjoram
¼ tsp. ground thyme
Paprika

Sauté onion in butter for 10 minutes or until tender. Add diced beef and all of the rest of the ingredients except paprika. Mix well. Turn into a casserole. Sprinkle generously with paprika and bake in a moderate over (350 degrees) for 30 minutes. Serves 6.

CHILI CON CARNE

4 c. canned red kidney beans | 2-½ c. canned tomatoes
2 lbs. ground beef | 4 tbsp. chili powder
2 c. onion, sliced | ½ tsp. red pepper, crushed
3 cloves garlic, minced | ¾ tsp. oregano
¼ c. oil | 1 tsp. salt

Sauté onion and garlic in oil for 10 minutes. Add beef, brown. Add other ingredients, cover, simmer for 30 minutes. Serves 6.

SCRAPPLE

1-½ lbs. pork shoulder | ¼ tsp. ground thyme
¼ lb. pork liver | 1 tsp. ground sage
1 c. yellow corn meal | 1 tsp. ground marjoram
¼ c. onion, finely chopped | 2 tsp. salt
¼ tsp. ground cloves | Freshly ground black pepper

Simmer meats in saucepan with 4 c. of water for 1 hour. Drain and save broth. Bone pork shoulder and chop shoulder and liver. Combine corn meal, salt, 1 c. cold water and 2 c. broth in saucepan. Cook, stirring until thickened. Add meat, onion, and spices. Cover and simmer for 1 hour. Pour scrapple into loaf pan (9" x 5" x 3"). Chill for 4 hours. To serve, slice, dip in flour and fry.

WHITE CHILI

1 lb. large white beans	6 c. chicken broth
2 cloves garlic, minced	2 onions, medium, chopped
1 tsp. oil	
2–4 oz. cans mild green chilies, chopped	
2 tsp. ground cumin	1-½ tsp. oregano
¼ tsp. ground cloves	¼ tsp. cayenne pepper
4 c. cooked chicken breasts, diced	
3 c. Monterey Jack cheese, grated	
Salsa	Sour Cream

Combine beans, broth, garlic, and half of the onions in a large soup pot. Bring to a boil. Reduce heat and simmer until beans are soft (2 hours or more), adding more broth or as necessary. In a skillet, sauté remaining onion in oil until tender. Add chilies and seasonings and mix thoroughly. Add to bean mixture. Add chicken and simmer 1 hour. Serve topped with grated cheese, salsa and sour cream. Serves 8 to 10.

STACY M^cCOY'S CHICKEN LASAGNA

4 c. chicken, cooked and shredded	
1 onion, chopped	
3 tbsp. olive oil	2 cloves garlic
1 green pepper, chopped (optional)	
1 c. mozzarella cheese	1 pint cottage cheese

Sauté onion, garlic, green pepper with oil in fry pan. Add chicken.

Sauce:

1 pint of half and half	Dash Italian seasoning

Simmer in the pan until warm and thick.

Combine: Layer lasagna noodles with chicken mixture; cottage cheese and mozzarella cheese, and tomato sauce in a baking dish. Bake at 350 degrees for 30 to 35 minutes or until cheese is bubbling.

– 6 –

CASSEROLES

NOTES

GERMAN BEEF CASSEROLE

1 lb. ground round, browned and drained
1 head cabbage, chopped
2 c. grated cheddar cheese
1 can tomato soup plus ½ can water

Place browned beef in bottom of casserole dish; layer with cabbage and cheese; pour tomato soup over top and bake for 30 minutes at 350 degrees.

SAUSAGE, PEAS, AND MUSHROOMS

Brown 1 lb. of sausage, drain well. Add 1 can of drained sliced mushrooms, 1 can peas, drained, 1 stick butter, and 1 tsp. garlic powder. Stir together and simmer for 10 minutes. Serve with mashed potatoes and cornbread.

TUNA CASSEROLE

2 cans white chunked tuna, drained and chipped
1 pkg. Kraft deluxe macaroni and cheese, cooked according to directions
1 onion, chopped
1 pkg. frozen peas, cooked and drained
1 can cream of mushroom soup
2 stalks celery, chopped

Stir all ingredients together and bake in covered casserole dish for 30 minutes at 350 degrees. Uncover and bake for 10 minutes on 400 degrees.

TOMATO CASSEROLE

6 medium tomatoes, chopped and cored
1 c. tomato ketchup   ½ c. sugar
1 c. plain croutons or seasoned
½ c. Parmesan cheese   1 c. shredded mozzarella

Butter a casserole dish, layer ingredients in dish and bake for 30 minutes on 350 degrees.

MIXED VEGETABLE CASSEROLE

1 bag frozen mixed vegetables, cooked
1 c. onions, chopped   1 c. mayo
1 c. sharp cheddar cheese   1 c. celery, chopped
1 c. breadcrumbs

Mix all ingredients together and top with breadcrumbs. Bake at 350 degrees for 30 minutes. Serve hot.

SAUSAGE-ONION TURKEY STUFFING

1 lb. hot sausage   2 c. celery, chopped
4 tbsp. butter   ½ tsp. lemon pepper
2 tsp. grated orange rind   ¼ c. chopped parsley
1 medium onion, minced   8 c. bread crumbs
2 tsp. salt   1 tsp. thyme
1 tsp. marjoram   1 tsp. sage
¼ c. orange juice   ¼ c. currants

Sauté celery and onion in butter. Soak currants in orange juice. Fry and drain sausage. Combine all ingredients and stuff into a 12 or 14 lb. turkey. Bake according to turkey directions.

SAUSAGE-GRIT CASSEROLE

1 lb. sausage
1 small onion, chopped
1-½ c. shredded sharp cheddar cheese

1 c. quick-cooking grits
⅓ c. chopped green pepper

Cook grits according to package directions. Set aside. Crumble sausage in large skillet; add onion and green pepper. Cover over medium heat until meat is browned and vegetables are tender, stir occasionally. Drain well. Combine grits, meat mixture, and 1 cup cheese. Spoon into lightly greased 10" x 6" x 2" baking dish. Bake at 350 degrees for 15 minutes. Sprinkle with remaining ½ cup of cheese; bake 5 minutes longer or until cheese melts. Makes 8 servings.

SOUTH OF THE BORDER CASSEROLE

1 lb. ground beef
8 oz. (2 c.) Land-o-Lakes 4 qt. Monterey Jack cheese,
cut into ½ inch cubes
½ c. (1 med.) finely chopped onion
2 (8 oz.) cans tomato sauce
8 oz. (1 c.) Land-o-Lakes lean cream
4 oz. can diced green chilies
⅓ c. shredded Land-o-Lakes 4 qt. cheddar cheese
8 oz. pkg. tortilla chips

Heat oven to 350 degrees. In 10-inch skillet cook beef and onion until meat is browned and onion is tender (8 to 10 minutes); drain. Add tomato sauce, chilies, and oregano. Cook over low heat for 10 minutes; remove from heat. In greased 2-½ quart casserole dish layer half of each of the following ingredients: tortilla chips, Monterey Jack cheese, and ground beef mixture. Repeat layering. Bake for 20 to 25 minutes or until heated through. Remove from oven, spread top with lean cream and sprinkle out edge with cheddar cheese. Bake just until cheese is melted (4 to 5 minutes). Serve immediately. Yields 6 to 8 servings.

PEA CASSEROLE

2 cans peas or 2 pkgs. frozen peas thawed
1 onion, diced   ½ green pepper
4 sticks celery, diced   ½ tsp. salt
½ stick butter   1 c. breadcrumbs
1 can cream of mushroom soup

Sauté above ingredients in ½ stick of margarine. Cover with breadcrumbs. Drain 2 cans of peas. Mix all with 1 can cream of mushroom soup. Bake at 350 degrees for 30 minutes.

MACARONI, CHEESE AND PEAS

1 box macaroni and cheese   3 stalks celery, chopped
1 pkg. frozen peas, thawed   4 boiled eggs, chopped
1 onion, chopped   ½ c. mayonnaise

Prepare macaroni and cheese according to directions on the box. Add the above ingredients and salt until will combined. Serve warm topped with crushed crackers or serve chilled.

MASHED POTATO CASSEROLE

In a greased baking dish layer the following ingredients:
3 c. mashed potatoes   3 small green onions, sliced
1 c. sour cream   1 (4 oz.) pkg. shredded cheese
5–6 slices bacon, fried crisp and crumbled

Bake at 300 degrees for 30 minutes.

BROCCOLI CASSEROLE

2 stalks celery, chopped   1 onion, chopped
½ stick butter   4 c. steamed broccoli, chopped
1 can golden mushroom soup or cream of celery soup
1 c. grated cheese   1 pkg. Ritz crackers, crushed

Sauté onion and celery in butter. Mix all ingredients and pour into greased casserole dish. Bake at 350 degrees for 25 minutes.

**Boneless chicken tenders, cooked; may be added to serve as main dish.

SCALLOPED POTATOES

6 to 8 medium red potatoes, washed and diced (do not peel)
1 large onion, chopped   1 stick butter, sliced into pats
1 green pepper, chopped   1 c. grated cheddar cheese
½ c. sour cream   ½ c. milk
Salt to taste   Pepper to taste

Stir all ingredients together and pour into greased casserole dish. Bake at 350 degrees for 1 hour. Stirring occasionally.

SQUASH CASSEROLE

3 c. squash, cooked, drained and mashed
¾ c. margarine   1 c. onion, chopped
1 tsp. salt   ½ tsp. pepper
2 eggs   1 c. milk
1 c. cheese   1 box stuffing

Mix ingredients together and pour into baking dish and bake at 375 degrees for 40 minutes.

CHICKEN POT PIE

Yield: 2 pies

3 c. cooked chicken breast, cubed
½ c. chicken broth
2/3 c. milk
⅓ c. margarine or butter
1 small onion, minced
⅓ c. flour
Salt and pepper
1 bag mixed vegetables, thawed

In a sauce pan, make a gravy with flour, butter, broth and milk. Add onion, salt and pepper. Mix all other ingredients and pour into unbaked pie crust. Top with crust and bake at 425° for 40 minutes.

NOTES

– 7 –

SALADS

NOTES

HEAVENLY HAM SALAD

3 c. finely chopped Heavenly Ham
½ c. mayo   3 tbsp. pickle relish
2 eggs, boiled and chopped
½ c. shredded cheese (your choice)

Stir all ingredients together and chill. Spread on toasted whole wheat bread.

SPAM SALAD

1 can Spam, shredded
½ c. shredded cheese (Velveeta or cheddar)
1 green pepper, finely chopped
1 onion, minced   2 boiled eggs, finely chopped
½ c. mayo   3 tbsp. pickle relish

Stir all ingredients together. Spread on fresh white bread sliced.

DUMBO SALAD

½ lb. bologna, shredded   ½ c. shredded cheese
3 eggs boiled, chopped   1 small onion, minced
1 c. mayo   4 tbsp. pickle relish

Stir ingredients together and spread on sliced fresh white bread.

TUNA SALAD

2 c. white chunk tuna, drained and chopped
1 green pepper, finely chopped
1 onion, minced   1 c. mayo
2 boiled eggs, chopped   1 tbsp. celery seed
1 tsp. Mrs. Dash   1 red pepper, finely chopped
1 carrot, grated   2 stalks celery, finely chopped
3 tbsp. pickle relish

Stir all ingredients together. Chill. Serve on toasted bread with fresh sliced tomato.

AUNT OLA MAE'S PRETZEL SALAD

Mix together 2 c. crushed pretzels, 4 tbsp. sugar, and ¾ c. melted butter, and spread in 9 x 13 pan; bake at 400 degrees for 6 minutes. Mix together 8 oz. cream cheese, and 1 (16 oz.) container Cool Whip and pour on top of cooled crust. Dissolve 1 large box strawberry jello in 2 c. boiling water. Take 2 (10 oz.) pkgs. frozen strawberries, mix with jello and let chill until congealed. Then spread over cream cheese mixture and keep refrigerated.

MOM'S JELLO FRUIT SALAD

2 large boxes strawberry jello, dissolved in 4 c. boiling water. Pour into 9 x 13 dish. Add 2 c. chopped apples, 1 c. chopped pecans, 1 (8 oz.) pkg. cream cheese, chopped. Chill until thickened, cut in squares to serve.

MOTHER'S PEA SALAD

2 cans peas, drained
1 c. mayo
1 green pepper, chopped
Salt and pepper to taste

5 boiled eggs, chopped
1 medium onion, chopped
1 tsp. paprika

Stir all ingredients together and chill before serving.

PASTA SALAD

1 pkg. rainbow pasta, cooked and drained
1 c. grated mozzarella cheese
1 c. finely chopped broccoli   1 c. finely chopped cauliflower
1 onion, finely chopped   1 green pepper, finely chopped
1 red pepper, finely chopped   1 c. diced ham

Dressing:
1 c. olive oil
1 tsp. celery seed
2 tbsp. vinegar
Salt and pepper to taste

1 tsp. minced garlic
½ c. Italian salad dressing
3 tbsp. sugar
½ c. mayonnaise

Mix dressing ingredients together until blended well. Pour dressing over noodles and veggies and mix well with hands. Chill well before serving.

CURRIED CHICKEN SALAD

Salad:
2 c. cooked, cubed chicken   ½ tsp. toasted silvered almonds
1-½ c. diagonally sliced celery
20 oz. can pineapple chunks, drained

Curry Dressing:
¾ c. Land-o-Lakes lean cream
½ tsp. curry powder
½ tsp. salt

Lettuce leaves if desired

In large bowl, stir together all salad ingredients except lettuce. Cover, refrigerate until chilled (2 to 3 hours). In a small bowl, combine all dressing ingredients. Cover, refrigerate. Just before serving, toss salad with dressing. If desired, serve on lettuce leaves. Yield 4 to 6 servings.

CHUNKY FRUIT SALAD

1 can chunky fruit cocktail   Maraschino cherries
1 can large chunk pineapple
1 pint container whipping cream, whipped
Grapes, sliced and seeded   Bananas, sliced
1 can mandarin oranges   Apples, sliced

Soak apples and bananas in 3 tbsp. lemon juice. Mix all fruits together. Add whipped cream and toss. Decorate with cherries and pecans.

DR. GOMEZ'S MEXICAN CHEF'S SALAD

Chop one onion, four tomatoes, and one head lettuce. Toss with 4 oz. grated cheddar cheese and 8 oz. of French dressing, add hot sauce to taste. Chill. Crunch and add one bag Doritos, dice and add one avocado.

Brown ground round and add 4 tbsp. of taco seasoning, add one can drained kidney beans, one tsp. salt, and simmer for 10 minutes. Mix with salad and serve Pronto!

QUICK FRUIT SALAD

1 large can fruit cocktail   1 can mandarin oranges
1 large can pineapple chunks   1 (3 oz.) box Jell-O (any flavor)
1 small carton cottage cheese 1 small container Cool Whip

Drain well, sprinkle one 3 oz. box Jell-O, any flavor, mix, and add one small container of Cool Whip and one small carton of cottage cheese. Mix well and chill for several hours before serving.

CICELY SHACH'S CURRY CHICKEN SALAD

2 c. mayo   1-½ c. chopped celery
2 tbsp. lemon juice   2 tbsp. soy sauce
1 (6 oz.) can water chestnuts, drained and sliced
1 rounded tbsp. curry powder
2 c. seedless grapes   1 tbsp. onion juice
1 lb. can pineapple chunks   3 c. diced chicken
½ c. slivered almonds

Combine mayo, lemon juice, soy sauce, onion juice, curry power, and chutney. Pour over chicken, celery, water chestnuts, grapes, and pineapple chunks. Toss well. Sprinkle almonds on top of salad.

MINNESOTA LAYER SALAD

1 head lettuce, broken
4 stalks celery, chopped
4 green onions, chopped
1 can water chestnuts, sliced
1 pkg. frozen peas, thawed
2 c. Hellman's mayonnaise
2 tbsp. sugar
Grated Romano chest

Place ingredients in large bowl in layers. Spread mayonnaise on top, sprinkle sugar, and cheese. Refrigerate 8 hours. May be garnished with bacon crumbles and sliced boiled egg.

CAESARS SALAD

2 heads romaine lettuce, ends and stalks snipped

Chop lettuce about 1 inch apart. Wash and role into clean dish towel. Refrigerate. In large bowl, place 1 egg, beat slightly. Add 2 cloves, minced; garlic; 2 tbsp. Dijon mustard; 1 tsp. red wine vinegar; 1 tsp. Worcestershire sauce; 3 minced anchovies; 1 tbsp. mayo, and 2 tbsp. olive oil. Mix well. Remove lettuce from refrigerator, toss in large bowl with dressing, top with croutons and serve. Diced tomatoes and fresh sliced mushrooms are optional.

AUNT ELOISE'S FRESH SPINACH SALAD

1 bag spinach, washed and torn
8 slices bacon, fried crisp and crumbled
1 small can bean sprouts, drained
1 small onion, sliced thin and separated into rings
1 small can water chestnuts, sliced thin
2 hard boiled eggs, chopped

Toss in a large bowl. Add dressing.

Dressing:
1 c. salad oil $\frac{1}{3}$ c. ketchup
$\frac{1}{2}$ c. wine vinegar   Dash of salt
$\frac{1}{2}$ c. sugar

Blend well and warm. Pour over tossed salad.

AUNT OLA MAE'S ORANGE ALMOND SALAD

$\frac{1}{2}$ c. salad oil   3 tbsp. wine vinegar
1 tbsp. lemon juice   2 tbsp. sugar
$\frac{1}{2}$ tsp. salt $\frac{1}{2}$ tsp. dry mustard
$\frac{1}{2}$ tsp. grated onion

Shake above ingredients in a jar and refrigerate for 1 hour.

1 (11 oz.) mandarin oranges, drained
1 bunch romaine, Boston, or leaf lettuce, washed and torn into small pieces
$\frac{1}{2}$ red onion, cut into rings
$\frac{1}{2}$ c. slivered almonds, toasted

Mix these ingredients in large salad bowl and pour refrigerated dressing on top. Toss. Serves 4 to 6 people.

LIME JELLO SALAD

1 box lime Jell-O
1 carrot, grated

1 onion, chopped
1 green pepper, chopped

Mix Jell-O according to box directions, let cool. Add the onion, green pepper, and carrot. Mix well. Chill until Jell-O has set. Cut into squares and serve over lettuce leaves topped with ½ tsp. mayonnaise.

PINEAPPLE SALAD

1 large can crushed pineapple
8 oz. box Jell-O (lemon, lime or strawberry)
1 pint buttermilk   1 c. Cool Whip

Mix Jell-O with crushed pineapple, juice included. Simmer pineapple and Jell-O. Cool. Pour buttermilk into mixture. Pour into bowl and stir in Cool Whip. Chill.

ALASKAN PEA SALAD

½ head chopped lettuce   1 c. Hellman's mayonnaise
1 c. frozen peas, thawed and drained
1 green pepper, chopped   1 red onion, chopped
½ c. Baco's
½ c. fresh grated Parmesan cheese

Layer lettuce, green peppers, peas, and onion in bowl. Top with mayonnaise and add Parmesan cheese and pour Baco's over top. Chill and cover with lid.

BLACK BEAN AND CORN SALAD

½ c. basic vinaigrette   ¼ tsp. seasoned pepper
¼ tsp. dried cilantro   ⅛ tsp. cayenne pepper
¼ tsp. ground cumin
2 (15-oz.) cans black beans, rinsed and drained
2 (15-oz.) cans whole kernel corn, drained
½ c. onion, chopped   ½ c. scallions, chopped
½ c. red bell peppers, chopped

In a small bowl, mix together vinaigrette, seasoned pepper, cilantro, cayenne pepper, and cumin. Set dressing aside. In a large bowl, stir together beans, corn, onion, scallions, and red bell pepper. Toss with dressing. Cover, and refrigerate overnight. Toss again before serving.

BRENDA'S PAPAW'S FRUIT SALAD

1 bag coconut   1 c. pecans
½ c. sugar   1 c. mayo
6 medium apples, diced   1 box white raisins
1 lb. white grapes
1 can crushed pineapple, drained
1 pint cottage cheese   1 jar cherries, maraschinos

Mix ingredients in a large bowl and serve over cottage cheese, topped with pecans and cherries.

STACY McCOY'S BROCCOLI SALAD

1 bunch broccoli, chopped   1 c. raisins
½ salted sunflower seed (unsalted optional)
6 slices bacon, crushed   1 small red onion, chopped

Wash broccoli and cut off half of stalk and discard. Cut the rest up small. Combine the rest of ingredients in a bowl.

Dressing:
½ c. mayo   2. tbsp. red wine vinegar
2 tbsp. sugar

Put dressing on just before serving and mix thoroughly.

MERRY CHRISTMAS SALAD

½ c. celery, chopped   ½ c. carrots, grated
1 cucumber, chopped   Salt and pepper to taste
Bread and Butter pickles, chopped
1 red pepper, chopped
6 green onions, chopped   1 c. cauliflower, chopped
1 box macaroni, cooked   1 c. mayo
1 c. cheddar cheese, shredded
6 eggs, boiled and chopped
Small bottle Zesty Italian Dressing

Prepare macaroni according to box instructions. Combine all ingredients in a large bowl and mix adding Italian Dressing as needed for consistency and taste. Served chilled.

LEX WRIGHT SALAD

Living in Mountain View, California, some 70 miles north of the Salinas Valley, Lex used as many as six different kinds of lettuce: red, Romaine, Boston, iceberg, etc. But in Kentucky, we make do with head lettuce. Sometimes we add green pepper strips, etc.

To the greens add onions (sliced green onions, or thin slices of hamburger onions) and tomatoes.

The dressing: equal numbers of 1) rounded tbsp. Hellman's mayonnaise, 2) wine vinegar, and 3) vegetable oil. Add garlic salt, salt, cracked pepper, Parmesan cheese AND liquid smoke. (Wright's, available at Winn-Dixie is the better).

Toss and Enjoy! –J. Wright, Warsaw, Kentucky

PASTA (SPAGHETTI) SALAD

1 lb. spaghetti, cooked   2 stalks celery, chopped
1 tbsp. celery seed   1 green pepper, chopped
½ cucumber, chopped fine   1 onion, chopped
½ pkg. pepperoni, quartered
Salad Seasoning, 1 envelope Italian Dressing
Parmesan cheese

Cook spaghetti 10 minutes. Combine all the ingredients in a bowl and toss lightly with the Italian dressing salad seasoning. Sprinkle with Parmesan cheese.

ASIAN COLE SLAW

1 bag broccoli cole slaw
1 pkg. beef ramen noodles, crunched. Add noodle seasoning to
1 cup sugar, ¾ c. apple cider or rice vinegar.
6 small green onions, sliced
1 c. almonds, sliced
1 c. sunflower kernels

Mix all ingredients in a large bowl. Chill one hour.

NOTES

− 8 −

SOUPS

NOTES

CORN BEEF CHOWDER

Boil:

10 potatoes, diced

3 c. water

Add:

1 c. chopped celery

1 c. chopped onion

1 can Pet milk (large)

1 stick butter

½ c. milk

1 can whole kernel corn

1 can corned beef or hash

2 bay leaves

After potatoes are done, add remaining ingredients and simmer until done.

AUNT OLA MAE'S CLAM CHOWDER

2 onions, chopped

½ stick butter

2-½ c. boiling water

½ tsp. pepper

1 can tomatoes

1 c. celery, diced

1 c. potatoes, diced

1 tsp. salt

½ tsp. thyme

2 cans minced clams, drained

Bring all ingredients except clams to boil for 30 to 45 minutes. Add clams, cook 20 additional minutes. Serve hot.

PAPAW'S BROCCOLI & LEEK SOUP

Chop 1 leek, 2 onions, 1 head broccoli; cook in 2 c. water until boiling. Add seasoned salt and pepper to taste, add ½ stick butter, 2 cloves, minced garlic, and remove from heat and cool slightly. Purée in food processor or blender, pour back into kettle. Add 1 quart half and half, 2 tbsp. cornstarch in 2 tbsp. melted butter. Pour into broccoli mixture and heat until thickened.

POTATO CHOWDER

6 medium potatoes, diced
4 stalks celery, diced
1 stick butter
2 bay leaves, crushed
Seasoned salt and pepper to taste

1 qt. boiling water
2 small onions, chopped
2 cans evaporated milk
1 tsp. salt

Bring all ingredients to boil, simmer 30 minutes. Add 1 can whole kernel corn. Fry 6 strips bacon, crisp, remove from skillet and crunch. Add 3 tbsp of flour to bacon grease in skillet, stir until thickened. Pour into chowder and slowly stir. Add crunched bacon. Simmer for 15 minutes and serve hot.

CHILI

2 lb. fresh ground round, browned and drained
2 c. water
4 tbsp chili powder
1 c. cooked pinto beans and 1 c. cooked red kidney beans
1 large onion, chopped
1 tsp. garlic powder
1 can tomato paste

1 can tomato sauce

1 can chili beans
1 tsp. tiger sauce

Simmer all ingredients together for 2 hours.

* If cooking chili for hot dog sauce, add tomato sauce into ground round while browning. Stir constantly. Also add 1 can Vietti's hot dog sauce.

FRENCH ONION SOUP

4 large onions   4 tbsp. butter
4 (10-½ oz.) can condensed beef broth
½ c. dry sherry   Dash pepper
2 tsp Worcestershire sauce
6 slices French bread, toasted, ½ " thick
¾ c. Parmesan cheese   6 slices Swiss cheese

Cook onion, butter, broth, sherry, pepper, and Worcestershire sauce for 20 minutes. Toasted bread topped with cheeses until melted. Place bread in soup bowls. Pour 1-½ cups soup into bowls and serve hot.

MEXICAN GOULASH

1 lb. ground beef, browned   ½ green pepper, chopped
1 medium onion, chopped   ½ can tomato paste
Dash chili powder   3 tomatoes, chopped
1 can whole kernel corn, drained

Stir all ingredients in large sauce pot and simmer over low heat for 25 minutes.

HOME CANNED SOUP MIX

Yellow squash   Tomato
Onion(s)   Zucchini
Green and Red Pepper   Celery

Chop all the above ingredients and add the following: 1 tsp. basil, 1 tsp. pickling salt to each quart. Put in quart jars. Pressure cooker: 5 minutes on 10 lbs.

ORIENTAL DUMPLING SOUP

4 c. chicken broth
1 pkg. (10 oz.) frozen Japanese-style vegetables
1 to 2 tbsp. soy sauce   1 tsp. lemon juice
1 c. cooked chicken, cubed   Dash of ginger
Dumplings:
½ c. all-purpose flour   1 egg
2 tbsp. milk

In large saucepan, combine chicken broth, soy sauce, lemon juice, vegetables, and chicken; bring to a boil. In small bowl, combine all dumpling ingredients; mix well. Drop batter by ½ tsp. into boiling liquid. Cook until dumplings float to surface and vegetables are tender, about 2 to 3 minutes. If desired, garnish each bowl with a thin lemon slice. Makes 4—½ cup servings.

COD CHOWDER

2 lbs. cod   1 bay leaf, crumbled
2 oz. salt pork, diced   1 qt. milk
2 onions, sliced   2 tbsp. butter
4 large potatoes, diced   1 tsp. salt
1 c. celery, chopped   Freshly ground black pepper

Simmer cod in 2 cups water for 15 minutes. Drain. Reserve broth. Remove bones from cod. Sauté diced pork until crisp, remove and set aside. Sauté onions in port fat until golden brown. Add cod. Potatoes, celery, bay leaf, salt and pepper. Pour in cod broth plus enough boiling water to make 3 cups of liquid. Simmer for 30 minutes. Add milk and butter and simmer for 5 minutes. Serve chowder sprinkled with pork dice. Serves 6.

LOBSTER BISQUE

1 lobster (about 1 lb.)
2 qt. fish stock or court bouillon

2 c. celery	2 c. onion
2 c. carrots	1-½ c. butter
½ c. flour	½ tsp. cayenne pepper
1 tbsp. paprika	1 c. heavy cream
Sherry	

Break apart the lobster by separating the main body from the tail. Split main body in half. Break off the claws. Clean the inside of the lobster. Put all parts into soup pot with fish stock. Cook for 10 to 15 minutes until lobster is bright red. When done, remove from pot and let cool. Remove all meat from shell, being sure to keep the meat in big pieces. Set aside meat.

Put shells back into the pot with the stock. Chop vegetables. In another pot, add chopped vegetables. Sauté in ½ c. butter. Don't let it burn. Add ½ c. flour to make a roux with the vegetables. Add cayenne pepper and paprika. Sauté. Let all mix well. Add the court bouillon to the vegetable mixture. Let simmer until thickened about 10 to 15 minutes. Purée mixture, shells included, in food processor. Strain through fine sieve to remove shell particles. Pour back into the soup pot and simmer on medium to medium-high heat. Add cream and whisk in 1 stick butter, at room temperature. Add sherry to taste. Add chopped lobster to soup and serve.

Shrimp may be substituted for the lobster. Sauté the shrimp, peel, and throw the shells into the court bouillon, then follow the same procedure as for the lobster bisque.

TOMATO SOUP

Purée 10–12 tomatoes, peeled and cored. Add 1 can tomato sauce and 1 can tomato soup, minced garlic, salt and paper, and a dash of basil. Cook for one hour. Serve hot or cold.

VEGETABLE SOUP

1 large soup bone with beef   ½ gallon water

Place soup bone in large pot and cover with water.
Add 4 stalks celery with leaves, 2 onions, chopped. 1 quart jar canned tomatoes or 2 (12 oz.) cans stewed tomatoes. Boil stock 15 minutes; turn down to medium heat. Add: 3 peeled, chopped potatoes, 1 bag Green Giant frozen mixed vegetables. 1 c. shredded cabbage, 1 can whole kernel corn, 2 carrots, peeled and sliced thin, salt and pepper to taste. Simmer 2 hours on low heat, stir occasionally.

– 9 –

VEGETABLES

NOTES

BAKED BEANS

2 cans (large) Bush's best baked beans
1 tbsp. Heinz 57 sauce   3 strips bacon, chopped
1 small can tomato paste   ½ c. black molasses
1 onion chopped   1 tbsp. yellow prepared mustard

Mix all ingredients together. Bake at 300 degrees for 2 hours. Stirring occasionally.

ALMOND GREEN BEANS

2 lb. fresh green beans (Tenderette)
Snip ends of beans and wash

In stir-fry skillet, stir-fry beans in 1 cup water, ½ cup olive oil, 2 cloves, minced garlic, and ½ stick butter. When beans are tender, and ¼ cup slivered almonds. Stir and serve.

STIR-FRY BEANS AND CARROTS

1 lb. green beans, snip ends and wash
4 large carrots, peeled, sliced lengthwise strips

Sauté in garlic butter (1 stick butter, 2 cloves garlic, minced) until tender. Add ½ c. water, cover and simmer for 15 minutes.

GARLIC PEAS AND MUSHROOMS

2 cans peas, drained   2 cans mushrooms, drained
2 tsp. garlic powder   ½ stick butter

This can be prepared in microwave oven. Stir together all ingredients in covered microwave dish. Heat on full power for 5 minutes.

BROCCOLI LASAGNA

1 head broccoli, cooked, chopped and drained
1 c. ricotta cheese   1 c. mozzarella cheese
1 c. cottage cheese   1 c. milk
1 clove garlic, minced   ½ stick butter
1 pkg. lasagna noodles, cooked and drained
Sliced onion   Parmesan cheese

Place broccoli, cheeses, and milk in blender or food processor and purée. Add 1 clove minced garlic; melted in ½ stick of butter to broccoli mixture. Starting with noodles, layer lasagna noodles and broccoli mixture in casserole dish until you have layered all the ingredients. Top with grated Parmesan cheese and sliced onion. Bake at 300 degrees for 1-½ hour.

MART'S DIRTY POTATOES

In greased baking dish, place sliced potatoes. Add seasoned salt and pepper to taste. Crumble 6 slices of fried bacon over the potatoes, sprinkle on garlic salt. Slice ½ stick butter over bacon. Chop 1 green pepper and 1 onion and sprinkle on top of butter. Top with 1 cup grated Velveeta cheese. Bake at 350 degrees for 1-½ hours.

SOUPERB RICE

Prepare 2 servings rice according to package directions, omitting salt and adding 1 envelope Lipton chicken noodle cup-a-soup with white meat. Makes 2 servings.

Variation:
Use 1 envelope Lipton onion, tomato, or spring vegetable cup-a-soup. Recipe can be doubled.

CREAMED EGGS

1 pkg. Pepperidge Farm pastry shell
1 c. cooked ham, cut in julienne strips
2 tbsp. butter or margarine
¼ c. sliced green onion   ½ c. chopped green pepper
2 tbsp. flour   2 c. milk
4 hard cooked eggs, sliced
1-½ cooked asparagus, cut into 1" pieces

Prepare pastry shells according to package directions. Meanwhile, brown ham in butter in saucepan. Add green pepper and onion and cook several minutes, stirring frequently until vegetables are tender. Add flour and cook stirring until bubbling and smooth. Remove from heat and stir in milk. Add eggs and asparagus and reheat. Spoon into hot pastry shells. Makes 6 servings.

SAUTÉED VEGETABLES

In a large skillet or wok, melt 1 stick butter, add 2 cloves minced garlic, and 1 c. water. Then add:
1 c. broccoli flowerets   1 yellow squash, sliced
1 c. cauliflower flowerets   1 c. mushrooms, sliced
1 c. snow peas   2 onions, sectioned
1 carrot, sliced   2 tomatoes, quartered
1 zucchini squash, sliced

Sauté above until tender (about 10 minutes on high).

BACON CHEEZY TATERS

5 potatoes, sliced thin   5 slices bacon, fried, crumbled
2 c. Velveeta cheese   1 onion, chopped
1 stick margarine   2 c. milk

Place all ingredients in well-greased casserole dish and bake for 1-½ hours at 350 degrees.

BACO BEANS

1 lb. fresh green beans or 2 cans cut green beans, drained
½ c. Baco's   1 small onion, chopped
2 tbsp. cooking oil

If using fresh beans, cover with water. If using canned beans, add 1 c. water. Seasoned salt and pepper to taste. Simmer beans for 1 hour.

SPINACH SOUFFLÉ

2 boxes, frozen, chopped spinach
1 small onion, minced   1 tsp. mace
3 eggs, slightly beaten   ½ c. heavy cream

Cook spinach, set aside, cool. Blend in beaten eggs, cream, mace, and onion. Pour into greased soufflé dish. Bake at 400 degrees 25 to 30 minutes.

ZUCCHINI MARINARA

3 small to medium zucchini, sliced thin
½ c. water   1 large onion, chopped
½ stick butter   2 small tomatoes, chopped
2 cloves garlic, minced

Sauté all ingredients in skillet, uncovered until almost dry. Cover, reduce heat, and simmer for 10 minutes. Serve hot.

ZUCCHINI PARMESAN

2 medium zucchini, sliced
1 tsp. basil
1 c. milk
Seasoned salt and pepper to taste

1 tsp. oregano
1 clove garlic, minced
1 c. Parmesan cheese, grated

Cook all ingredients together in saucepan, covered on medium heat until zucchini is tender, stirring occasionally.

FLAVORED TATERS

Prepare 2 servings instant mashed potatoes according to package directions, omitting salt and adding ¼ cup additional liquid. Stir in 1 envelope Lipton cream of mushroom or cream of chicken flavor cup-a-soup. Makes 2 servings. Use more or less as desired. Recipe can be doubled.

BROCCOLI AND RICE

1 pkg. chopped broccoli
1 c. chopped celery
1 small onion, chopped
1 tsp. salt

½ c. uncooked rice
1 small jar Cheese Whiz
1 can cream of celery soup

Cook together: broccoli, celery, onion and salt until tender. Cook rice separately. Mix and add Cheese Whiz and soup. Pour into buttered dish and bake at 350 degrees for 30 minutes.

POTATOES AU GRATIN

5 potatoes, chunked
1 c. sour cream

1 c. cheddar cheese
1 c. half and half

Put in casserole dish in order above and bake for 1 hour at 350 degrees.

BUTTERY SWEET CARROTS

½ c. sugar
1 tsp. tarragon

1 stick butter
1 tsp. allspice

1 can carrots or about 6 fresh carrots, sliced thin

Put into saucepan with 1 c water and cook over medium heat for about 20 minutes.

SEASONED CAULIFLOWER

Sprinkle cauliflower with seasoned salt and pepper, cover with squeeze margarine and steam until tender.

SAUTÉED MUSHROOMS

1 large pkg. whole mushrooms, washed and dried.

In sauce pot, melt 1 stick butter, add 2 cloves minced garlic, 1 c. red wine, 1 c. water, 1 medium onion, diced. Bring to boil, add mushrooms. Simmer on low heat for 30 minutes. Serve hot. Great with steaks.

JERRY HUNTER'S STUFFED SQUASH

8 or 10 small yellow squash   1 small onion, grated
2 slices Roman Meal Bread, crumbled
½ c. butter   Salt and pepper to taste
Paprika

Parboil squash to tender; hull out inside. Mix inside with onion, bread crumbs, butter, and season with salt and pepper. Fill shells with this mixture. Top with grated cheese and paprika. Bake in 350 degree oven for 20 to 30 minutes. I sometimes add Parmesan cheese too.

COMPANY CABBAGE

1 medium head cabbage, chopped
15 oz. can cream   ¼ c. water
4 tbsp. flour   4 tbsp. butter
½ c. green pepper, diced   ½ c. pimento
½ c. sharp cheese, cubed   Parmesan cheese, sprinkled

Cook cabbage until translucent, drain. Mix with other ingredients and sprinkle Parmesan cheese on top. Bake at 350 degrees for 30 minutes.

SWEET PICKLES

Quarter or slice
1 peck cucumbers   1 c. pickling salt

Place in ice water for 12 hours or overnight.

Mix:
6 tsp. celery seed   6 tsp. mustard seed
3-½ c. white distilled vinegar   4 c. sugar

Bring to boil and pour over cucumbers in clean dry, jars and seal.

MOUNTAIN KRAUT

12 qt. jars stuffed with shredded cabbage
1 gal. water   1 c. salt
½ c. vinegar

Bring liquid to a boil. Pour over full jar and add more cabbage if needed. Seal.

VEGGIE BARS

¼ mayo   1 pkg. (8 oz.) cream cheese
1 pkg. Hidden Valley Ranch Dressing
¾ c. each: cauliflower, broccoli, and carrots, chopped fine
1 tomato, chopped   1 c. cheddar cheese, shredded
1 pkg. crescent rolls

Mix mayo, cream cheese, and dressing. Stir in the vegetables. Top with tomato and cheddar cheese. Spread crescent dough into a 9 x 13" pan. Layer the pan with the mixture and top with tomato and cheddar cheese. Bake in a 375 degree oven for 13 to 15 minutes.

FREEZER SLAW

6 lbs. cabbage, shredded   3 tbsp. salt
3 stems celery, chopped   2 bell peppers, chopped
5-½ c. sugar   2 c. water
2-½ c. white vinegar   1 tbsp. celery seed
1 tbsp white mustard seed

Sprinkle cabbage with salt. Stand 1 hour and add celery and green pepper. Stand 20 minutes. Drain well. On stove, combine all other ingredients. Bring to boil and pour over cabbage. Mix well. Place in freezer bags.

AUNT LORETTA'S COLORFUL CRISPY COLESLAW

1 sm. cabbage, shredded (about 1-½ lb.)*
1 medium onion, chopped
1 carrot, scraped and shredded
1 sm. green pepper, chopped
1 sm. sweet red pepper, chopped
1 sm. sweet yellow pepper, chopped
1 c. sugar**
1 c. + 2 tbsp. vinegar
½ c. vegetable oil
1 tsp. salt   ¼ tsp. ground white pepper
1 tsp. celery seeds   ¼ tsp. mustard seeds

Combine first 7 ingredients in a large bowl; stir well. Cover and chill for 2 hours. Combine vinegar, oil, salt, pepper, celery seeds, and mustard seeds in a saucepan; bring to a boil, stirring until salt dissolves. Pour vinegar mixture over cabbage mixture; toss gently. Cover and chill at least 2 hours. Serve with a slotted spoon. Yield: 6 to 8 servings.

Note: Coleslaw will keep in the refrigerator several days.

*In place of small cabbage I use three 10 oz. pkgs. of shredded cabbage.
**In place of sugar, I use 24 pkgs. of Equal.

BROCCOLI WITH HERB BUTTER

3 lbs. broccoli   ¼ tsp. oregano
¼ c. butter   ¼ tsp. salt
4 tbsp. lemon juice   Freshly ground black pepper
1 garlic clove, minced

Trim heavy, coarse stalks from broccoli. Steam broccoli spears for 20 minutes or until tender. Combine and heat remaining ingredients and pour over broccoli. Serves 6.

BOSTON BAKED BEANS

2 c. dried navy beans
½ lb. salt pork, halved
½ c. dark molasses

2 tsp. onion, grated
½ tsp. dry mustard

Soak beans overnight in water to cover. Bring to a boil in the same water, reduce heat, cover and simmer for 1 hour. Drain, save water. Put half of pork in 6-cup bean pot. Add beans, molasses, onion, mustard, and ½ cup bean water. Put other pork half on top. Cover and bake in a slow oven (300 degrees) for 5 hours, adding bean water if needed. Uncover, bake for 1 hour. Serves 6.

KIDNEY BEANS IN RED WINE

2 c. dried red kidney beans
1 c. dry red wine
4 slices bacon, cut up
1 tbsp. onion, grated

2 tbsp. butter
2 tbsp. flour
1 tsp. salt
Freshly ground black pepper

Soak beans overnight in water to cover. Simmer them in the soaking water with bacon and salt for 2 hours. Drain beans and keep them hot. Sauté onion in butter for 5 minutes. Add flour and pepper and stir until smooth. Add wine and cook until thickened, stirring constantly. Add to beans and mix well. Serves 6. Black beans may be substituted for red kidney beans. Four cups of canned kidney beans, heated and drained, may be used instead of 2 cups of dried beans, soaked and cooked.

JILL'S MAPLE BACON GREEN BEAN BUNDLES

1 bag frozen whole green beans, rinsed with hot water and dried
1 pkg. (1 lb.) maple bacon
1 stick butter   2 tbsp. garlic, minced
½ c. brown sugar

Half-fry the pkg. of bacon, place on paper towel to drain and cool. Bundle about 10 to 12 beans with the bacon as a wrap held together with a toothpick. Place bundles into a 9 x 13 baking dish. Melt the stick of butter with the minced garlic and drizzle over the beans. Sprinkle with brown sugar. Bake in a 350 degree oven for 30 minutes.

HASH BROWN CASSEROLE

2 pkgs. frozen hash browns
½ can cream of celery soup
½ can cream of chicken soup
4 large spoons of sour cream
1 onion minced
1 c. shredded Swiss cheese
1 c. shredded cheddar cheese
4 large spoons of mayonnaise

Bake at 325° for one hour. Top with crunched corn flakes.

NOTES

– 10 –

BREAKFAST FOODS

DEB'S OLD FASHIONED OATMEAL PANCAKES

2 c. old fashioned oats   2 tbsp. sugar
2 c. buttermilk   1 tsp. baking powder
2 large eggs   1 tsp. baking soda
¼ c. butter or margarine, melted and cooled
½ tsp. ground cinnamon
⅓ c. dark seedless raisins   ½ tsp. salt
½ c. flour

Mix oats and buttermilk in a large bowl. Cover and refrigerate. When ready to cook, beat in eggs and butter. Stir in raisins. Mix flour, sugar, baking powder and soda, cinnamon and salt. Add to oat mixture and stir briskly just until moistened. If possible, let batter stand 20 minutes or so before cooking. Heat a lightly greased griddle or frying pan over medium heat. Pour about ¼ cup of batter onto griddle for a "test" cake. If batter seems too thick, add more buttermilk, one tbsp. at a time (up to 3 tbsp.). Cook until a few bubbles appear on tops; turn to brown other side. Makes 18 pancakes.

CRANBERRY SYRUP

1–12 oz. can frozen cranberry juice cocktail concentrate, undiluted
¼ tsp. fresh-grated lemon peel
Few grains cinnamon and nutmeg
2 tbsp. cornstarch mixture with 1 tbsp. water

Bring cranberry juice, lemon peel and spices to boil. Stir in cornstarch mixture, boil one minute. Serve warm. (You can add more cornstarch depending on desired thickness.)

GARLIC OMELET WITH HOT RED PEPPER

4 cloves garlic
½ tsp. salt
1 tbsp. olive oil
¼ tsp. red-pepper flakes

8 eggs
¼ tsp. pepper
1 tbsp. butter

Cut the garlic into slivers. Whisk the eggs, garlic, salt, pepper, and 2 tbsp. of cold water until mixed. Warm the oil and butter in a 10" omelet or frying pan over medium heat. When the butter begins to foam, turn the heat to medium-high and pour in the egg mixture. With a fork, draw the edges of the eggs toward the middle and tilt the pan so that the uncooked egg flows underneath. Continue until the omelet is just set and the top is creamy moist, about 4 minutes. Take the pan from the heat at once and loosen the omelet edges with a fork. Fold the omelet in half and turn out on warm platter. Sprinkle with red-pepper flakes and serve.

QUICK 'N SPECIAL OMELET

1 envelope Lipton cream of chicken or
cream of mushroom cup-a-soup
3 tbsp. milk   Butter or margarine
2 eggs

In bowl, blend cup-a-soup, eggs, and milk. In omelet pan or skillet, melt butter, add egg mixture. With spatula, lift set edges of omelet, tilting pan to allow uncooked mixture to flow to bottom. When omelet is set, but still slightly moist, fold in half and serve. Makes 1 serving

CINNAMON PIZZA

Top a ready crust with cinnamon, sugar and butter. Bake at 375° until golden brown.

*Both these recipes were given to me by my dad,
Leonard McCoy, the best hillbilly chef in
the state of Kentucky.*

APPLE SOUFFLÉ PANCAKES

Slice 3 medium peeled apples into half moon slices. Boil apples in ½ cup water for 3 to 5 minutes, set aside.

Pancake batter:

2 c. flour   2 egg whites
1 c. milk

Beat egg whites until stiff. Stir pancake batter until smooth and fold in egg whites and stir. In a small skillet, place apples 3 to 5 slices; pour batter over top apples, cook over medium heat until bottom is done. Place in heated broiler oven and brown the tops. Serve with hot syrup and lots of butter.

BANANA CREPES

Crepe Batter:

1 c. flour
½ c. milk
1 egg

3 bananas, sliced in half

Beat with mixer until thin. In greased crepe pan, fry 2 tbsp. batter until done. Cooking on both sides until golden brown. Roll ½ of sliced banana into crepe. Keep in warm oven while preparing others. This recipe makes about 6 crepes. Serve with hot syrup.

BLUEBERRY WAFFLES

2 c. plain flour or whole wheat flour
2 eggs
1 c. milk

Mix well until fluffy. Pour into greased waffle iron and cook until crispy done. Top with fresh blueberries and hot maple syrup.

FRENCH TOAST

10 slices Texas toast bread
2 tsp. cinnamon
2 tbsp. half and half

6 eggs, beaten
Dash nutmeg (optional)

Mix cinnamon, nutmeg, eggs, and mil together, whip until fluffy. Dip bread into egg mixture until coated well on both sides. Pop onto hot buttered griddle and fry until golden brown. Serve with hot syrup. Sprinkle with confectioner's sugar.

GOOD EGGS

6 to 8 eggs, beaten

Chop 1 medium onion, ½ c. green pepper, ½ c. red pepper. Sauté in ½ stick butter. Pour beaten eggs into greased skillet; add sautéed veggies, and ½ c. grated cheddar cheese and ¼ c. grated Swiss cheese. Stir constantly until eggs are scrambled and cheeses are melted. Serve with toasted English muffins and hash browns. You can also add chopped, cooked ham or cooked sausage.

FRIED APPLE PIES

3 c. plain flour
¾ c. dry milk
1 stick butter flavored Crisco in 2 c. hot water

Knead together. Roll out onto floured bench and cut dough about the size of your hand.

Apple Filling:
10 medium to large apples (yellow delicious are best) peeled and chopped. ½ c. syrup, 1 c. sugar, dash of cinnamon and nutmeg. Cook on low until it resembles applesauce (this gets sticky).

Place one serving spoon size of apple filling in dough and pinch ends together. (I use a fork to mash the dough tight.) Fry and flip in iron skillet until golden brown—using butter flavored Crisco or plain shortening. Drain on paper towels.

BREAKFAST PIZZA

1 pizza crust (all ready or boxed)
1 lb. sausage browned
4–6 eggs, scrambled
1 onion, minced
1–2 cloves garlic, minced
4 small plum tomatoes, sliced

Top crust with sausage, onion, garlic, and tomato. Pour eggs over and bake at 400° twenty minutes or until golden brown.

– 11 –

SAUCES, RELISHES, CONDIMENTS

NOTES

VANILLA SAUCE

To be served over fresh strawberries or mixed fruit.

In double boiler, place 3 egg yolks, 1 pint half & half, ½ c. sugar. Stir with wire whisk and cook until thickened. Add ½ tsp. vanilla and 1 dash fresh grated nutmeg.

ALL-AMERICAN MUSHROOM SAUCE

1 envelope Lipton cream of mushroom cup-a-soup
½ c. boiling water
¼ to ⅓ c. shredded American cheese

In small bowl, blend all ingredients. Serve over hot cooked vegetables or pasta. Makes about ¾ cup sauce.

Substitution: Use 2 to 3 slices American cheese

SOUPER CREATE-A-GRAVY

In bowl, blend 2 envelopes Lipton cream of chicken flavor or cream of mushroom cup-a-soup with 1 cup boiling water. Serve over hot cooked nooks, rice, beef, fish, or poultry. Makes about 1 cup gravy.

Variations: Add one of the following:
2 tbsp. white wine; 1 tbsp. sherry; 2 tsp. parmesan cheese; ½ tsp. dill weed or 1 hard-cooked egg, chopped and ½ tsp. parsley.

ITALIAN HERB DRESSING

8 oz. carton Land-o-Lakes lean cream
¼ tsp. salt   ½ tsp. basil leaves
⅛ tsp. pepper   ½ tsp. oregano leaves
2 tsp. lemon juice

In a small bowl, stir together all ingredients. Cover, refrigerate 1 to 2 hours. Yield: 1 cup.

BÉARNAISE SAUCE

Dash of Worcestershire sauce   ¼ lb. butter, melted
4 tbsp. tarragon vinegar   3–4 tbsp. tarragon leaves
3 or 4 egg yolks

Mix leaves with vinegar and boil down to ⅔. Add this mixture to egg yolks. Heat in double boiler, whipping constantly with wire whip. Add melted butter a little at a time.

HORSERADISH SAUCE

1 stick butter   1 c. horseradish
1 onion   ¼ c. vinegar
2–3 tbsp. flour, stir into butter ¼ c. sugar

Brown onion in butter. Add water until you get the consistency you want. Season with salt and pepper.

TAB'S SALAD DRESSING

1 tsp. lemon juice
1 tsp. vinegar
1 c. mayonnaise
2 tbsp. red wine
2 tbsp. olive oil

1 egg yolk
1 tbsp. honey
1 tsp. Dijon mustard
2 cloves garlic, minced

Mix well.

TEN HUNDRED ISLAND DRESSING

Daddy's version Thousand Island Dressing.

1 boiled egg, chopped
1 c. mayonnaise
2 tbsp. chili sauce

1 tbsp. pickle relish
1 tbsp. green pepper, chopped

Mix all ingredients together and pour over salad.

IRENE STANLEY'S SPAGHETTI SAUCE

½ bushel of tomatoes
5 to 6 small bell peppers or 3 large ones
3 lbs. onions
1 c. sugar
1 pint cooking oil
4 to 5 hot banana peppers
Black pepper to taste (I use 1 tbsp.)
3 tbsp. garlic, chopped

4 tbsp. oregano
½ c. canning salt
1 tbsp. basil
5 (12-oz.) cans tomato paste

Peel tomatoes, place in large roaster pan, chopped with hand cabbage cutter, cook. Grind peppers and onions in grinder or food processor. Add ingredients to cooked tomatoes, bring to boil and cook for 2 to 3 hours, stirring occasionally. You may can or freeze mixture. When you open the jars, brown ground beef or other meat and add sauce. **Delicious!**

MS. ATCHISON'S APPLE BUTTER

16 c. apple pulp; or 16 c. peeled apples, chopped and mashed
1 c. dark vinegar   8 c. sugar
1 pkg. red hots

Cook in a crock pot overnight or bake in an oven at 250 degrees. Can the next morning.

APPLE BUTTER

8 qts. apples, chopped
2 c. hot water   1 c. vinegar
30 oz. cinnamon imperial's candies
10 c. sugar

Set oven to bake at 300 degrees. Bake chopped apples two hours. Add all ingredients to canner, cook until apples resemble apple sauce. Spoon into clean jars and seal.

SWEET PEPPER JELLY

10 medium bell peppers, diced
3 banana peppers, diced   2 red peppers, diced
½ c. cider vinegar   5 c. sugar
1 box sure jell or pectin

Wash and chop peppers. Prepare lids and jars. Measure exact amounts. Stir pectin or sure jell into peppers and vinegar. Bring to a boil, add sugar at full rolling boil. Boil exactly 1 minute. Reduce heat to medium high stirring constantly for 10 minutes. Ladle into jars while hot. Yields 6 pints.

WEST VIRGINIA PEPPERS

Quarter green pepper, red peppers, etc. Measure to amount in tomato sauce. Add fresh basil. Cook on low heat together and place in jars and boil in water for 15 minutes.

MARINADE FOR RIBS

Brush ribs with olive oil.
Seasoning Rub: 1 tbsp. each garlic, onion, seasoned salt, and pepper. Seal ribs with plastic foil. Roll in foil 3 to 4 times, marinade overnight. Remove wrap and BBQ on grill until done about 30 to 45 minutes.

FLORENE'S CHOCOLATE GRAVY

1 c. flour
$\frac{1}{3}$ c. cocoa

1 c. sugar
5 c. water

Mix all ingredients together with one cup cold water. Put 4 cups of water on to boil. When it comes to a boil, pour into other mixture.

GARLIC SAUCE

6 garlic cloves, sliced
1 c. olive oil
1 c. butter
1 tsp. fresh parsley, chopped

1 tsp. basil
$\frac{1}{2}$ tsp. oregano
1 tsp. salt
Freshly ground black pepper

Sauté garlic in combined olive oil and butter for 5 minutes. Add parsley, basil, oregano, salt and pepper and simmer for 5 minutes, stirring constantly. Makes about 2 cups.

TARRAGON MARINADE

3 tbsp. tarragon vinegar
2 large onions, sliced
1 lemon
5 garlic cloves, split
1 bay leaf

¼ tsp. dry mustard
½ c. dry red wine
1 c. olive oil
Freshly ground black pepper

Line a shallow glass baking dish or a wooden trough with some onion slices. Squeeze lemon juice over the onion, toss in the lemon rinds. Add garlic, spices, salt, and pepper. Pour in vinegar, wine, and oil. Lay a steak in the marinade and spread the rest of the onion slices on the steak. Marinate for 3 hours, basting frequently. This amount is enough for 2 pounds of 2-inch sirloin. Serve the marinated onions raw with the cooked steak.

DIANE SAUCE FROM STANLEY DEMOS

1 large spoon bacon grease
2 big dashes of each: A1, honey, Worchestershire sauce, Heinz 57, Dijon mustard
1 cup sliced mushrooms
1 onion chopped

Cook in skillet with meat drippings.

RED WINE SAUCE

2 cloves minced garlic
1 large onion, minced
2 tbsp. butter

Saute in a skillet over medium heat until golden. Add 4 tbsp. tomato paste and 3 cups red wine. Simmer 15 minutes.

– 12 –

HANDY TIPS & TRICKS

STEP-BY-STEP
INSTRUCTIONS FOR
HOME CANNING

1. Select quality ingredients at their peak of freshness; prepare them according to a tested recipe. Assemble jars, lids, bands, and canning equipment. Check all items to ensure they are in good working condition.

2. Process Acid foods in a boiling-water canner. Acid foods include: Jellies, Jams, Preserves, Marmalades, and other Soft Spreads. Fruits, Tomatoes (with added acid), Pickles, Relishes, and Chutneys.

3. Process Low-Acid food in a steam-pressure canner. Low-Acid foods include: Vegetables, Meats, Poultry, Seafood, and Combination Recipes (with acid and low-acid ingredients).

4. Wash jars, lids and bands in hot, soapy water. Rinse well. Dry bands and set aside. Heat jars and lids in hot water (180° F), keeping them hot until used. Do not boil lids. (For recipes requiring less than 10 minutes processing, sterilize jars by boiling them for 10 minutes. At elevations higher then 1,000 feet above sea level, add 1 minute for each 1,000-foot increase.)

5. Fill hot jar with prepared recipe. Leave recommended headspace: ¼-inch for Fruit Juices, Pickles, and Soft Spreads; ½-inch for

fruits and tomatoes; 1-inch for Vegetables, Meats, Poultry, and Seafood.

6. Remove air bubbles by sliding a non-metallic spatula between the jar and food to release trapped air. Repeat procedure 2 to 3 times around jar.

7. Wipe rim and threads of jar with a clean, damp cloth. Center heated lid on jar with sealing compound next to glass. Screw band down evenly and firmly until a point of resistance is met—fingertip tight.

8. Place jar in canner. Repeat procedure for filling jars until the canner is full. Process filled jars following the method and processing time indicated by a tested recipe.

9. When processing time is complete, cool canner according to manufacturer's instructions. Remove jars from canner; set them upright on a towel to cool. Bands should not be retightened. Let jars cool 12 to 24 hours.

10. After jars are cool, test for a seal by pressing the center of the lid. If the lid does not flex up and down, the lid is sealed. Remove bands. Wipe jars and lids with a clean, damp cloth. Label and store jars in a cool, dry, dark place.

A HANDY SPICE AND HERB GUIDE

ALLSPICE: a pea-sized fruit that grows in Mexico, Jamaica, Central, and South America. Its delicate flavor resembles a blend of cloves, cinnamon, and nutmeg. USES: (Whole) Pickles, meats, boiled fish, and gravies; (Ground) Puddings, relishes, fruit preserves, baking.

BASIL: the dried leaves and stems of an herb grown in the United States and North Mediterranean area. Has an aromatic, leafy flavor. USES: For flavoring tomato dishes and tomato paste, turtle soup; also used in cooked peas, squash, snap beans; sprinkle chopped over lamb chops and poultry.

BAY LEAVES: the dried leaves of an evergreen grown in the eastern Mediterranean countries. Has a sweet herbaceous floral spice note. USES: For pickling, stews, for spicing sauces and soup. Also used with a variety of meats and fish.

CARAWAY: the seed of a plant grown in the Netherlands. Flavor that combines the tastes of anise and dill. USES: For the cordial Kummel, baking breads; often added to sauerkraut, noodles, cheese spreads. Also adds zest to french fried potatoes, liver canned asparagus.

CURRY POWDER: a ground blend of ginger, turmeric, and fenugreek seed, as many as 16 to 20 spices. USES: For all Indian curry recipes such as lamb, chicken, and rice, eggs, vegetables, and curry puffs.

MACE: the dried covering around the nutmeg seed. Its flavor is similar to nutmeg, but with a fragrant, delicate difference. USES: (Whole) For pickling, fish, fish sauce, stewed fruit. (Ground) Delicious in baked goods, pastries, and doughnuts, adds unusual flavor to chocolate desserts,

MARJORAM: an herb of the mint family, grown in France and Chile. Has a minty-sweet flavor. USES: In beverages, jellies, and to flavor soups, stews, fish, sauces. Also excellent to sprinkle on lamb while roasting.

MSG (MONOSODIUM GLUTAMATE): a vegetable protein derivative for raising the effectiveness of natural food flavors. USES: Small amounts adjusted to individual taste, can be added to steaks, roasts, chops, seafoods, stews, soups, chowder, chop suey, and cooks vegetables.

OREGANO: a plant of the min family and a species of marjoram of which the dried leaves are used to make an herb seasoning. USES: An excellent flavoring for any tomato dish, especially pizza, chili con carne, and Italian specialties.

PAPRIKA: a mild, sweet red pepper growing in Spain, Central Europe, and the United States. Slightly aromatic and prized for brilliant red color. USES: A colorful garnish for pale foods, and for seasoning Chicken Paprika, Hungarian Goulash, and salad dressings.

POPPY: the seed of a flower grown in Holland. Has a rich fragrance and crunchy, nut-like flavor. USES: Excellent as a topping for breads, rolls, and cookies. Also delicious in buttered noodles.

ROSEMARY: an herb (like a curved pine needle) grown in France, Spain, and Portugal, and having a sweet fresh taste. USES: In lamb dishes, in soups, stews, and to sprinkle on beef before roasting.

SAGE: the leaf of a shrub grown in Greece, Yugoslavia, and Albania. Flavor is camphoraceous and minty. USES: For meat and poultry stuffing, sausages, meat loaf, hamburgers, stews, and salads.

THYME: the leaves and stems of a shrub grown in France and Spain. Has a strong, distinctive flavor. USES: For poultry seasoning, croquettes, fricassees, and fish dishes. Also tasty on fresh sliced tomatoes.

TURMERIC: a root of the ginger family, grown in India, Haiti, Jamaica, and Peru, having a mild, ginger-pepper flavor. USES: As a flavoring and coloring in prepared mustard and in combination with mustard as a flavoring for meats, dressings, and salads.

CALCULATING FAT PERCENTAGE

To achieve a desirable percentage of total calories from fat, it is helpful to know how much fat is in individual foods. To determine the percentage of a food's total calories that come from fat, you can use the following formula. In order to calculate this percentage, you need to know the total calories and the grams of fat per serving, both of which are usually listed on the food label.

$$\frac{\text{grams of fat x } 9^*}{\text{total calories}} \text{ x } 100 = \begin{array}{l}\text{\% of total}\\\text{calories}\\\text{from fat}\end{array}$$

Each gram of fat contains 9 calories. Multiplying grams of fat by 9 gives the total calories from fat. On food labels, this number has already been calculated and is listed on the same line as total calories.

When reading a food package, the front of the label may not tell the whole story. For instance, a package of boiled ham might claim to be 96% fat free. From this information, the consumer might assume that the food contains 4% fat, which is well within the recommended guidelines of eating foods with 30% or less of total calories from fat.

Although the 96% fat free claim is truthful, it refers to the amount of fat by weight rather than by the food's total calories. To get a clearer picture, use the above calculation. The label of the boiled ham shows 60 calories and 2.5 grams of fat per serving.

$$\frac{2.5 \text{ grams of fat x } 9}{60 \text{ total calories}} \text{ x } 100 = \begin{array}{l} 37\% \text{ of total} \\ \text{calories} \\ \text{from fat} \end{array}$$

By calculating the percentage of total calories from fat, you can make more informed decisions about the nutritional qualities of foods. In this case, the ham may be lower in fat than other ham products, but it is still above the 30% guideline. If you are trying to follow a lowfat diet, you should eat this food in moderation.

HANDY CHART OF KITCHEN MATH WITH METRIC

KITCHEN MATH WITH METRIC TABLES

MEASURE	EQUIVALENT	METRIC (ML)
1 tablespoon	3 teaspoons	14.8 milliliters
2 tablespoons	1 ounce	29.6 milliliters
1 jigger	1½ ounces	44.4 milliliters
¼ cup	4 tablespoons	59.2 milliliters
⅓ cup	5 tablespoons plus 1 teaspoon	78.9 milliliters
½ cup	8 tablespoons	118.4 milliliters
1 cup	16 tablespoons	236.8 milliliters
1 pint	2 cups	473.6 milliliters
1 quart	4 cups	947.2 milliliters
1 liter	4 cups plus 3 tablespoons	1,000.0 milliliters
1 ounce (dry)	2 tablespoons	28.35 grams
1 pound	16 ounces	453.59 grams
2.21 pounds	35.3 ounces	1.00 kilogram

SIMPLIFIED MEASURES

"T" represents a tablespoon. "t" represents a teaspoon.

Dash = less than ⅛ tsp.	2 pts. (4 C.) = 1 qt.
3 tsp. = 1 T.	4 qts. (liquid) = 1 gal.
16 T. = 1 C.	8 qts. (solid) = 1 peck
1 C. = ½ pt.	4 pecks = 1 bushel
2 C. = 1 pt.	16 oz. = 1 lb.

If you want to measure part-cups by the tablespoon, remember:

4 T. = ¼ C.	10 ⅔ T. = ⅔ C.
5 ⅓ T. = ⅓ C.	12 T. = ¾ C.
8 T. = ½ C.	14 T. = ⅞ C.

THE APPROXIMATE CONVERSION FACTORS FOR UNITS OF VOLUME

TO CONVERT FROM	TO	MULTIPLY BY
teaspoons (tsp.)	milliliters (ml)	5
tablespoons (T.)	milliliters (ml)	15
fluid ounces (fl. oz.)	milliliters (ml)	30
cups (C.)	liters (l)	0.24
pints (pt.)	liters (l)	0.47
quarts (qt.)	liters (l)	0.95
gallons (gal.)	liters (l)	3.8
cubic feet (ft^3)	cubic meters (m^3)	0.03
cubic yards (yd^3)	cubic meters (m^3)	0.76
milliliters (ml)	fluid ounces (fl. oz.)	0.03
liters (l)	pints (pt.)	2.1
liters (l)	quarts (qt.)	1.06
liters (l)	gallons (gal.)	0.26
cubic meters (m^3)	cubic feet (ft^3)	35
cubic meters (m^3)	cubic yards (yd^3)	1.3

WEIGHTS & MEASURES

Liquid:
16 cups per gallon

Dry or Household Measures:
8 lbs. per 16 cups
16 tbsp. per cup
6 tbsp. per ⅓ cup
1 cup sugar per ½ lbs.
33 cups per 50 lbs.

CONTENTS OF CANS

Of the different sizes of cans used by commercial canners, the most common are:

SIZE	AVERAGE CONTENTS
8 ounces	1 cup
picnic	1 ¼ cups
No. 300	1 ¾ cups
No. 1 tall	2 cups
No. 303	2 cups
No. 2	2 ½ cups
No. 2 ½ cups	3 ½ cups
No. 3	4 cups
No. 10	12 to 13 cups

OVEN TEMPERATURES

Slow	300°
Slow Moderate	325°
Moderate	350°
Quick moderate	375°
Moderately hot	400°
Hot	425°
Very hot	475°

DEEP-FAT FRYING TEMPERATURES WITHOUT A THERMOMETER

A 1-inch cube of white bread will turn golden brown:

345° to 355°	65 seconds
355° to 365°	60 seconds
365° to 375°	50 seconds
375° to 385°	40 seconds
385° to 395°	20 seconds

COMMON BAKING DISHES & PANS

Spring Form Pan

Layer Cake or Pie Pan

Ring Mold

Baking or Square Pan

Loaf Pan

Brioche Pan

Angel Cake Pan

Bundt Tube

Equivalent Dishes

4-CUP BAKING DISH
= 9″ pie plate
= 8″ x $1^1 _4$″ layer cake pan
= $7^3 _8$″ x $3^5 _8$″ x $2^1 _4$″ loaf pan

6-CUP BAKING DISH
= 8″ or 9″ x $1^1 _2$″ layer cake pan
= 10″ pie pan
= $8^1 _2$″ x $3^5 _8$″ x $2^5 _8$″ loaf pan

8-CUP BAKING DISH
= 8″ x 8″ x 2″ square pan
= 11″ x 7″ x $1^1 _2$″ baking pan
= 9″ x 5″ x 3″ loaf pan

10-CUP BAKING DISH
= 9″ x 9″ x 2″ square pan
= $11^3 _4$″ x $7^1 _2$″ x $1^3 _4$″ baking pan
= 15″ x 10″ x 1″ flat jelly roll pan

12-CUP BAKING DISH OR MORE
= $13^1 _2$″ x $8^1 _2$″ x 2″ glass baking dish
= 13″ x 9″ x 2″ metal baking pan
= 14″ x $10^1 _2$″ x $2^1 _2$″ roasting pan

Total Volume of Pans

TUBE PANS
$7^1 _2$″ x 3″ Bundt tube	6 cups
9″ x $3^1 _2$″ fancy or Bundt tube	9 cups
9″ x $3^1 _2$″ angel cake pan	12 cups
10″ x $3^3 _4$″ Bundt tube	12 cups
9″ x $3^1 _2$″ fancy tube mold	12 cups
10″ x 4″ fancy tube mold	16 cups
10″ x 4″ angel cake pan	18 cups

SPRING FORM PANS
8″ x 3″ pan	12 cups
9″ x 3″ pan	16 cups

RING MOLDS
$8^1 _2$″ x $2^1 _4$″ mold	$4^1 _2$ cups
$9^1 _4$″ x $2^3 _4$″ mold	8 cups

BRIOCHE PAN
$9^1 _2$″ x $3^1 _4$″ pan	8 cups

COMMON CAUSES OF FAILURE IN BAKING

BISCUITS

1. Rough biscuits caused from insufficient mixing.
2. Dry biscuits caused from baking in too slow an oven and handling too much.
3. Uneven browning caused by cooking in dark surface pan (use a cookie sheet or shallow bright finish pan), too high a temperature and rolling the dough too thin.

MUFFINS

1. Coarse texture caused from insufficient stirring and cooking at too low a temperature.
2. Tunnels in muffins, peaks in center and soggy texture are caused from over mixing.
3. For a nice muffin, mix well but light and bake at correct temperature.

CAKES

1. Cracks and uneven surface may be caused by too much flour, too hot an oven and sometimes from cold oven start.
2. Cake is dry may be caused by too much flour, too little shortening, too much baking powder, or cooking at too low a temperature.
3. A heavy cake means too much sugar has been used or baked too short a period.
4. A sticky crust is caused by too much sugar.
5. Coarse-grained cake may be caused by too little mixing, too much fat, and too much baking powder, using fat too soft, and baking at too low a temperature.

6. Cakes fall may be caused by using insufficient flour, under baking, too much sugar, too much fat, or not enough baking power.
7. Uneven browning may be caused from cooking cakes at too high a temperature, crowding the shelf (allow at 2" around pans) or using dark pans (us bright finish, smooth bottomed pans).
8. Cake has uneven color is caused from not mixing well. Mix thoroughly, but do not over mix.

PIES

1. Pastry crumbles caused by over-mixing flour and fat
2. Pastry is tough caused by using too much water and over mixing dough.
3. Pies do not burn—for full or custard pies use a Pyrex pie pan or an enamel pan and bake at 400° to 425°

BREADS (YEAST)

1. Yeast bread is porous—this is caused by over-rising or cooking at too low a temperature.
2. Crust is dark and blisters—this a caused by under-rising, the bread will blister just under the crust.
3. Bread does not rise—this is caused from over-kneading or from using old yeast.
4. Bread is streaked—this is caused from under-kneading and not kneading evenly.
5. Bread baked uneven—caused by using old dark pans, too much dough in pan, crowding the oven shelf or cooking at too high a temperature.

SUBSTITUTIONS

FOR:	YOU CAN USE:
1 T. cornstarch	2 T. flour OR 1½ T. quick cooking tapioca
1 C. cake flour	1 C. less 2 T. all-purpose flour
1 C. all-purpose flour	1 C. plus 2 T. cake flour
1 square chocolate	3 T. cocoa and 1 T. fat
1 C. melted shortening	1 C. salad oil (may not be substituted for solid shortening)
1 C. milk	½ C. evaporated milk and ½ C. water
1 C. sour milk or buttermilk	1 T. lemon juice or vinegar and enough sweet milk to measure 1 C.
1 C. heavy cream	⅔ C. milk and ⅓ C. butter
1 C. heavy cream, whipped	⅔ C. well-chilled evaporated milk, whipped
Sweetened condensed milk	No substitution
1 egg	2 T. dried whole egg and 2 T. water
1 tsp. baking powder	¼ tsp baking soda and 1 tsp. cream of tartar OR ¼ tsp baking soda and ½ C. sour milk, buttermilk or molasses; reduce other liquid ½ C.
1 C. sugar	1 C. honey; reduce other liquid ¼ C; reduce baking temperature 25°
1 C. miniature marshmallows	About 10 large marshmallows, cut up
1 medium onion (2½ dia.)	2 T. instant minced onion OR 1 tsp. onion powder OR 2 tsp. onion salt; reduce salt 1 tsp.
1 garlic clove	⅛ tsp. garlic powder OR ¼ tsp. garlic salt; reduce salt ⅛ tsp.
1 T. fresh herbs	1 tsp. dried herbs OR ¼ tsp. powdered herbs OR ½ tsp. herb salt; reduce salt ¼ tsp.

FAT FACTS

Reducing fat in diets is a major focus in America today, and for good reason. A high fat diet can contribute to elevated blood cholesterol levels, a risk factor for heart disease. Excess dietary fat has also been linked to obesity and cancer. As a result, lower fat intake has become a priority for many.

Cholesterol is a fat-type substance found in all animal tissues. In adults, a blood cholesterol level below 200 milligrams per deciliter is desirable. A level above 240 milligrams is considered high. Blood cholesterol can also be broken into two categories: "good" and "bad" cholesterol. High density lipoproteins (HDL) are known as "good" cholesterol because of their high protein content and low cholesterol content, and because people with higher HDL levels have a lower incidence of heart disease. Low density lipoproteins (LDL) contain more cholesterol than HDL and are responsible for cholesterol build-up on artery walls, thus earning the label "bad" cholesterol. A lowfat, low cholesterol diet, as well as exercise and being at a desirable weight, can help lower blood cholesterol levels and raise HDL levels.

Dietary fat can be divided into three different types: saturated, poly-unsaturated, and monounsaturated. Foods we eat contain a mixture of these fats.

- **Saturated fats** are generally solid at room temperature. They have been shown to increase blood cholesterol levels. Saturated fats are primarily found in animal products such as butter, milk, cream, and lard. Some plant foods, such as palm oil, coconut oil, vegetable shortening, and some peanut butters also contain large amounts of polyunsaturated fats.

continued on next page

- **Polyunsaturated fats** tend to lower blood cholesterol levels. These fats are found in high concentrations in vegetable oils, and are usually liquid at room temperature. Fats such as sunflower oil, corn oil, and soft margarines have large amounts of polyunsaturated fats.

- **Monounsaturated fats** have also been shown to decrease cholesterol levels in the blood. They can be liquid or solid at room temperature, and can be from plant or animal sources. Olive, peanut, and canola oils are high in monounsaturated fats.

- **Dietary cholesterol** comes from animal sources such as meat, poultry, fish, and other seafood, and dairy products. Egg yolks and organ meats contain high amounts of dietary cholesterol.

- **Hydrogenation** is a chemical process in which hydrogen is added to unsaturated oils to make them firmer at room temperature. Hydrogenated fats such as shortening or margarine are more saturated than the oil from which they are made. When choosing margarine, pick one with 2 grams or less saturated fat per tablespoon.

Heart Healthy guidelines include:
1. Limit total fat intake to 30% or less of total calories.
2. Of these calories, up to one-third can be saturated fat, and the remaining two-thirds should come from polyunsaturated and monounsaturated sources.
3. Limit daily cholesterol intake to 300 milligrams or less.

FOOD LABELING DEFINITIONS

Government regulations give specific guidelines as to what words can be used on a food label to describe the product. Here is a list of these descriptive terms.

FREE A produce must contain no amount or only an insignificant amount of one or more of the following: fat, saturated fat, cholesterol, sodium, sugar, and calories. The terms *no, without,* and *zero* can also be used.

Calorie-free: less than 5 calories per serving
Sugar-free or Fat-free: less than 0.5g per serving
Sodium-free: less than 5mg per serving

LOW This term can be used when referring to one or more of the following: fat, cholesterol, sodium, and calories. The terms *little, few,* and *low source of* can also be used.

Low calorie: 40 calories or less per serving
Lowfat: 3g or less per serving
Low saturated fat: 1g or less per serving
Low cholesterol: less than 20mg per serving
Low sodium: less than 140mg per serving
Very low sodium: less than 35mg per serving

LEAN meat, poultry, and seafood containing less than 10g of fat, less than 4g saturated fat, and less than 95g of cholesterol per 3.5 oz. serving.

HIGH One serving of a product must contain 20% or more of the *Daily Value* (recommended daily intake of a nutrient).

continued on next page

GOOD SOURCE On serving must contain 10% to 19% of the Daily Value.

REDUCED A nutritionally altered product containing 25% less of a nutrient or of calories than the regular product. If the regular product already meets the criteria for *low*, a *reduced* claim cannot be made.

LESS A food that contains 25% less of a nutrient or of calories than a similar food. Cream cheeses that have 25% less fat than butter could use the term *less* or *fewer.*

LIGHT This term can still be used to describe food characteristics such as color and texture if the label makes the meaning clear; for example, *light brown sugar.*

The term also carries two other meanings:
- A nutritionally altered product that contains one-third less calories or half the fat of the original food
- A food's sodium content has been cut by 50% or more

MORE A food using this claim must contain 10% more of the Daily Value of a nutrient than the reference food. To use the words *fortified, enriched,* or *added*, this standard must also be met.

UNSALTED, NO SALT ADDED, or WITHOUT ADDED SALT The sodium naturally found in the product is still there, but it has been prepared without the salt that is normally added.

FOOD SAFETY GUIDELINES

Food safety is an important part of food preparation. Bacteria that cause food-borne illnesses are present in many foods. Fortunately, with proper handling and cooking of foods, the danger from these bacteria and the toxins they may produce can be greatly reduced.

Follow these safety guidelines to help protect against food-borne illnesses:

- Keep the temperature in the refrigerator 35° F. or below.

- Thaw all meat, fish, or poultry in the refrigerator. Do not thaw on the kitchen counter. For faster thawing, a microwave can be used, but meat should be cooked immediately after thawing. Cook all meat and poultry thoroughly. The following chart is a guide.

FOOD	MINIMAL INTERNAL TEMPERATURE
Ground Meat	160° F.
Ground Poultry	165° F.
Beef, Veal, Lamb	145° F.
Pork	160° F.
Poultry	170° F.

- Cook fish until it is opaque, firm and flakes easily with a fork.

- Cook eggs until the white is set and the yolk is starting to thicken. Do not eat raw eggs or those

continued on next page

with cracks in the shell. Separate the egg white from the yolk by using an egg separator or a slotted spoon rather than by using the shell.

- Once cooked, hold food at temperature below 40° F. or above 140° F. Do not allow perishable food to sit between these temperatures for more than two hours. This is considered the *danger zone* at which bacteria can readily grow or produce toxins.

- Cool foods such as soups, sauces, and gravies in shallow pans no more than two inches deep.

- Keep raw animal products and their juices separate from other foods.

- Place raw meat on a plate or pan in the refrigerator to keep juices from dripping on other foods.

- Wash kitchen surfaces, utensils, and hands after they have been exposed to raw meat, poultry, fish, and eggs.

- Thoroughly clean cutting boards used for raw meat before using them for cooked foods or foods to be eaten raw, such as salad greens.

- Use a clean container to hold cooked meat. Do not reuse the container that held the raw meat without cleaning it first.

- When roasting a turkey or chicken with stuffing, it is best to cook the stuffing in a separate pan instead of in the cavity of the bird. If you choose to stuff the bird, however, do so just prior to putting it in the oven. When checking for doneness, make sure a thermometer placed into the center of the stuffing reads at least 165° F.

FOOD QUANTITIES FOR 25, 50, AND 100 SERVINGS

FOOD	25 SERVINGS	50 SERVINGS	100 SERVINGS
Rolls	4 doz.	8 doz.	16 doz.
Bread	50 slices or 3–1-lb. loaves	100 slices or 6–1-lb. loaves	200 slices or 12–1-lb. loaves
Butter	½ lb.	¾ to 1 lb.	1½ lb.
Mayonnaise	1 c.	2 to 3 c.	4 to 6 c.
Mixed filling for sandwiches (meat, eggs, fish)	1½ qt.	2½ to 3 qt.	5 to 6 qt.
Mixed filling (sweet fruit)	1 qt.	1¾ to 2 qt.	2½ to 4 qt.
Jams & preserves	1½ lb.	3 lb.	6 lb.
Crackers	1½ lb.	3 lb.	6 lb.
Cheese (2 oz. per serving)	3 lb.	6 lb.	12 lb.
Soup	1½ gal.	3 gal.	6 gal.
Salad dressings	1 pt.	2½ pt.	½ gal.
Meat, Poultry, or Fish:			
Wieners (beef)	6½ lb.	13 lb.	25 lb.
Hamburger	9 lb.	18 lb.	35 lb.
Turkey or chicken	13 lb.	25–35 lb.	50–75 lb.
Fish, large whole (round)	13 lb.	25 lb.	50 lb.
Fish, fillets or steaks	7½ lb.	15 lb.	30 lb.
Salads, Casseroles, Vegetables:			
Potato salad	4¼ qt.	2¼ gal.	4½ gal.
Scalloped potatoes	4½ qt. or 1–12" x 20" pan	8½ qt.	17 qt.

continued on next page

FOOD	25 SERVINGS	50 SERVINGS	100 SERVINGS
Mashed potatoes	9 lb.	18–20 lb.	25–35 lb.
Spaghetti	1¼ gal.	2½ gal.	5 gal.
Baked beans	¾ gal.	1¼ gal.	2½ gal.
Jello salad	¾ gal.	1¼ gal	2½ gal.
Canned vegetables	1–#10 can	2½–#10 cans	4–#10 cans
Fresh Vegetables:			
Lettuce (for salads)	4 heads	8 heads	15 heads
Carrots (3 oz. or ½ c. per serving)	6¼ lb.	12½ lb.	25 lb.
Tomatoes	3 to 5 lb.	7 to 10 lb.	14 to 20 lb.
Desserts:			
Watermelon	37½ lb.	75 lb.	150 lb.
Fruit cup (½ c. per serving)	3 qt.	6 qt.	12 qt.
Cake	1–10"x12" sheet cake or 1½–10" layer cakes	1–12"x20" sheet cake or 3–10" layer cakes	2–12"x20" sheet cake or 6–10" layer cakes
Whipping cream	¾ pt.	1½ to 2 pt.	3 pt.
Ice Cream:			
Brick	3¼ qt.	6½ qt.	12½ qt.
Bulk	2¼ qt.	4½ qt. or 1¼ gal.	9 qt. or 2½ gal.
Beverages:			
Coffee	½ lb. and 1½ gal.water	1 lb. and 3 gal. water	2 lb. and 6 gal. water
Tea	1/12 lb. and 1½ gal. water	1/6 lb. and 3 gal. water	1/3 lb. and 6 gal. water
Lemonade	10–15 lemons, 1½ gal. water	20–30 lemons, 3 gal. water	40–60 lemons, 6 gal. water

GLOSSARY OF FRENCH COOKING TERMS
Dedicated to my Aunt Jo

- **Amandine:** with almonds
- **Bombe:** ice cream
- **Bourguignon:** red wine sauce and garnish of mushrooms, little onions, and Lardoons (fried bacon)
- **Bigarade:** Orange and lemon sauce with many variations, particular for duck
- **Bercy:** baked with white wine, shallots, parsley and butter
- **Coquille:** shell shaped dish
- **Coq:** chicken
- **Chanterelles:** mushrooms
- **Diable:** deviled with white wine, vinegar, shallots, etc.
- **Dijonnaise:** sauce of chopped, hard cooked egg, Dijon mustard, oil and lemon juice beat up like mayonnaise
- **Jubile/cherries jubilee:** syrup simmered cherries with kersh (cherry wine) on top that is aflame when served
- **Lyonnaise:** white sauce of butter, onion, wine vinegar and stock
- **Ala Madrilène:** clear soups or other foods served cold and flavored with tomato juice
- **Marsala:** dessert wine of grapes used as aperitif before meals and in cooking
- **Morilles:** Morel mushrooms
- **Ala Montamorency:** dishes with cherries added to them
- **Marquery:** in buttered pan lines with pork skin, carrots and onions cut into rings
- **Moutarde:** mustard in cream sauce
- **Ala Mormande:** braised in white wine, usually fish
- **Ala Normande:** for chicken or meat—cider and calvados
- **Parisienne:** sauce of Gervais cheese, salt, paprika, beat with oil and lemon juice and chervil like a mayonnaise
- **Provencal:** sauce of oil, vinegar, salt, pepper, chopped tomatoes, hardboiled eggs, capers, gherkins, parsley and a little garlic
- **Paupiettes:** thin slices of beef or other meat stuffed with some forcemeat, rolled into cork shapes, wrapped in bacon and braised

"HEART HEALTHY" RECIPE SUBSTITUTIONS

ORIGINAL INGREDIENT	ALTERNATIVE	TF	SF	C
1 pound ground beef	• 1 pound ground turkey	X	X	X
1 ounce Cheddar, Swiss or American cheese	• 1 ounce low-fat cheese	X	X	X
	• 1 ounce part-skim cheese (Mozzarella)	X	X	X
1 egg	• 2 egg whites	X	X	X
	• ¼ c. low cholesterol egg substitute	X	X	X
1 c. whole milk	• 1 c. skim milk	X	X	X
1 c. cream	• 1 c. evaporated skim milk	X	X	X
1 c. sour cream	• 1 c. nonfat sour cream	X	X	X
	• 1 c. plain nonfat yogurt	X	X	X
	• 1 c. lowfat cottage cheese plus 1 to 2 tsp. lemon juice, blended smooth	X	X	X
1 oz. cream cheese	• 1 oz. nonfat cream cheese	X	X	X
	• 1 ounce Neufchatel cheese	X	X	X
1 c. butter	• 1 c. margarine		X	X
	• 1 c. vegetable oil		X	X
1 c. shortening	• 7 oz. vegetable oil		X	

KEY:
TF = total fat
SF = saturated fat

1 ounce baking chocolate	• 3 tbsp. cocoa powder plus 1 tbsp. vegetable oil		X	
Roux: 1 part fat 1 part starch	• ½ part fat to 1 part starch	X		
1 can condensed cream soup	• Mix together: ½ c. nonfat dry milk 2 tbsp. cornstarch 2 tsp. low sodium chicken bouillon ¼ tsp. onion powder ¼ tsp. garlic powder ¼ tsp. basil ¼ tsp. thyme ¼ tsp. white pepper 9 oz. cold water • ADD the following if desired: ¼ c. chopped celery or ½ c. sliced mushrooms • Heat to a boil, stir frequently. Per "can": 215 calories, 1g fat, 8mg cholesterol, 200mg sodium	X	X	X

LOW SODIUM SEASONING SUGGESTIONS

	Allspice	Basil	Bay Leaves	Caraway Seeds	Celery Seed	Chives	Curry Powder	Dill	Garlic	Ginger	Dry Mustard	Onion Powder	Oregano	Rosemary	Sage	Tarragon	Thyme
Beef	X									X	X				X	X	
Pork				X					X						X		X
Veal			X				X			X				X			X
Ground Meat	X	X			X				X		X						
Poultry			X				X			X				X		X	
Fish						X	X	X								X	
Eggs					X		X							X	X		
Soups/Stews	X	X	X	X	X				X			X					X
Sauces		X												X		X	
Pasta				X													
Rice		X					X					X					
Popcorn								X									
Asparagus				X													
Beets				X													
Broccoli											X		X				
Cabbage				X				X									
Carrots			X	X													
Cauliflower							X									X	
Green Beans								X			X						
Lima Beans						X	X								X		
Potatoes										X					X		X
Tomatoes		X					X		X				X				
Salads				X		X							X				

Try this low sodium spice blend in your shaker instead of salt:

1 tbsp. dry mustard
1 tsp. garlic powder
1½ tbsp. onion powder
½ tbsp. ground pepper
½ tbsp. thyme, crushed

1 tsp. sage
½ tsp. marjoram, crushed
1 tbsp. paprika
½ basil, crushed
½ tsp. ground oregano

MEAT ROASTING GUIDE

Cut	Weight Pounds	Approx. Time (Hours) (325° oven)	Internal Temperature
Beef			
Standing rib roast (10 inch) ribs (If using shorter cut (8 inch) ribs, allow 30 min. longer)	4	1¾	140° (rare)
		2	160° (medium)
		2½	170° (well done)
	8	2½	140° (rare)
		3	160° (medium)
		4½	170° (well done)
Rolled ribs	4	2	140° (rare)
		2½	160° (medium)
		3	170° (well done)
	6	3	140° (rare)
		3¼	160° (medium)
		4	170° (well done)
Rolled rump (Roast only if high quality. Otherwise, braise)	5	2¼	140° (rare)
		3	160° (medium)
		3¼	170° (well done)
Sirloin tip (Roast only if high quality. Otherwise, braise)	3	1½	140° (rare)
		2	160° (medium)
		2¼	170° (well done)
Lamb			
Leg	6	3	175° (medium)
		3½	180° (well done)
	8	4	175° (medium)
		4½	180° (well done)
Veal			
Leg (piece)	5	2½ to 3	170° (well done)
Shoulder	6	3½	170° (well done)
Rolled shoulder	3 to 5	3 to 3½	170° (well done)

POULTRY ROASTING GUIDE

Type of Poultry	Ready-To-Cook Weight	Oven Temperature	Approx. Total Roasting Time
Turkey	6 to 8 lb.	325°	2½ to 3 hr.
	8 to 12 lb.	325°	3 to 3½ hr.
	12 to 16 lb.	325°	3½ to 4 hr.
	16 to 20 lb.	325°	4 to 4½ hr.
	20 to 24 lb.	300°	5 to 6 hr.
Chicken (Unstuffed)	2 to 2½ lb.	400°	1 to 1½ hr.
	2½ to 4 lb.	400°	1½ to 2½ hr.
	4 to 8 lb.	325°	3 to 5 hr.
Duck (Unstuffed)	3 to 5 lb.	325°	2½ to 3 hr.

Note: Small chickens are roasted at 400° so that they brown well in the short cooking time. They may also be done at 325° but will take longer and will not be as brown. Increase cooking time 15 to 20 minutes for stuffed chicken and duck.

MICROWAVE HINTS

1. Place an open box of hardened brown sugar in the microwave oven with 1-cup hot water. Microwave at high for 1½ to 2 minutes for ½ pound or 2 to 3 minutes for 1 pound.

2. Soften hard ice cream by microwaving at 30% power. One pint will take 15 to 30 seconds; one quart, 30 to 45 seconds; and one-half gallon, 45 seconds to one-minute.

3. One stick of butter or margarine will soften in 1 minute when microwaved at 20% power.

4. Soften one 8-ounce package of cream cheese by microwaving at 30% power for 2 to 2½ minutes. One 3-ounce package of cream cheese will soften in 1½ to 2 minutes.

5. Thaw frozen orange juice right in the container. Remove the top metal lid. Place the opened container in the microwave and heat on high power 30 seconds for 6 ounces and 45 seconds for 12 ounces.

6. Thaw whipped topping…a 4½ ounce carton will thaw in 1 minute on the defrost setting. Whipped topping should be slightly firm in the center but it will blend well when stirred. Do not over thaw!

7. Soften jello that has set up too hard – perhaps you were to chill it until slightly thickened and forgot it. Heat on a low power setting for a very short time.

8. Dissolve gelatin in the microwave. Measure liquid in a measuring cup, add jello and heat. There will be less stirring to dissolve the gelatin.

9. Heat hot packs in a microwave oven. A wet fingertip towel will take about 25 seconds. It depends on the temperature of the water used to wet the towel.

10. To scald milk, cook 1-cup milk for 2 to 2½ minutes, stirring once each minute.

11. To make dry bread crumbs, cut 6 slices bread into ½-inch cubes. Microwave in 3-quart casserole 6-7 minutes, or until dry, stirring after 3 minutes. Crush in blender.

12. Refresh stale potato chips, crackers, or other snacks of such type by putting a plateful in the microwave oven for about 30-45 seconds. Let stand for 1 minute to crisp. Cereals can also be crisped.

13. Melt almond bark for candy or dipping pretzels. One pound will take about 2 minutes, stirring twice. If it hardens while dipping candy, microwave for a few seconds longer.

14. Nuts will be easier to shell if you place 2 cups of nuts in a 1-quart casserole with 1 cup of water. Cook for 4 to 5 minutes and the nutmeats will slip out whole after cracking the shell.

15. When thawing hamburger meat, the outside will many times begin cooking before the meat is completely thawed. Defrost for 3 minutes, then remove the outside portions that have defrosted. Continue defrosting the hamburger, taking off the defrosted outside portions at short intervals.

16. To drain the fat from hamburger while it is cooking in the microwave oven (one pound cooks in 5 minutes on high), cook it in a plastic colander placed inside a casserole dish.

17. Cubed meat and chopped vegetables will cook more evenly if cut uniformly.

18. When baking large cakes, brownies, or moist bars, place a juice glass in the center of the baking dish to prevent a soggy middle and ensure uniform baking throughout.

19. Since cakes and quick breads rise higher in a microwave oven, fill pans just half full of batter.

20. For stamp collectors: Place a few drops of water on stamp to be removed from envelope. Heat in the microwave for 20 seconds and the stamp will come right off.

21. Using a round dish instead of a square one eliminates overcooked corners when baking cakes.
22. When preparing chicken in a dish, place meaty pieces around the edges and the bony pieces in the center of the dish.
23. Shaping meatloaf into a ring eliminates under-cooked center. A glass set in the center of a dish can serve as the mold.
24. Treat fresh meat cuts for 15 to 10 seconds on high in the microwave oven. This cuts down on meat-spoiling types of bacteria.
25. A crusty coating of chopped walnuts surrounding many microwaved-cooked cakes and quick breads enhances the looks and eating quality. Sprinkle a layer of medium finely chopped walnuts evenly onto the bottom and sides of a ring pan or Bundt cake pan. Pour in batter and microwave as recipe directs.
26. Do not salt foods on the surface as it causes dehydration (meats and vegetables) and toughens the food. Salt the meat after you remove it from the oven unless the recipe calls for using salt in the mixture.
27. Heat leftover custard and use it as frosting for a cake.
28. Melt marshmallow crème in the microwave oven. Half of a 7-ounce jar will melt in 35-40 seconds on high. Stir to blend.
29. Toast coconut in the microwave. Watch closely because it browns quickly once it begins to brown. Spread ½ cup coconut in a pie plate and cook for 3-4 minutes, stirring every 30 seconds after 2 minutes.
30. Place a cake dish up on another dish or on a roasting dish or on a roasting rack if you have difficulty getting the bottom of the cake done. This also works for potatoes and other foods that do not quite get done on the bottom.

SODIUM

Sodium is a mineral used by the body to maintain a proper balance of water in the blood. Although it is a vital nutrient, the body needs very little sodium to stay healthy. Because it is found naturally in some foods and is added to many other foods, getting too little sodium is usually not a problem. A high sodium diet, on the other hand, can contribute to high blood pressure in some people. Reducing sodium intake in the diet may help prevent or control high blood pressure. It is hard to know who will develop high blood pressure, or who might benefit from eating less sodium. For these reasons, and because most individuals consume much more sodium than needed, it is generally suggested that we reduce sodium intake.

Table salt is the major source of sodium in our diet. It is made up of about half sodium and half chloride. An adult diet containing between 1,100mg and 2,300mg of sodium per day is considered adequate. One teaspoon of salt contains 2,000mg of sodium

Ways to Reduce Dietary Sodium

• Taste food before salting. Salt food only sparingly at the table.

• Cut back on sodium slowly to give the body time to adjust to less salty flavors. Salt-craving taste buds will eventually be replaced by new ones that do not have an affinity for salt.

• Choose foods that have little or no sodium added. In general the more processed the food, the more sodium it contains. For example, processed turkey breast purchased at a deli has considerably more sodium than fresh turkey breast.

- In many recipes, the salt can be cut back or even eliminated without greatly affecting the taste. Experiment with recipes at home, using less salt each time and using low sodium substitutes for high sodium ingredients.

- Read labels on food packages. Compare the sodium content to similar items and to the recommended sodium intake for an entire day.
- Limit intake of high sodium foods such as cheeses, processed meats, soups, broths, snack foods, canned vegetables, and vegetables juices, pickled vegetables, gravies, sauces, commercial casserole mixes, frozen dinners, and condiments. In many cases, lower sodium alternatives are available.

- When eating in restaurants, ask for foods to be prepared without added salt, and request to have sauces, gravies, dressings, and condiments served on the side.

- Use herbs and spices instead of salt to enhance the flavor of foods. Check the label of seasonings to be sure they do not contain sodium. Use onion powder rather than onion salt, garlic powder instead of garlic salt. In place of seasoning salt, try commercially prepared herb and spice blends or make your own.

SUGGESTIONS FOR LOWERING FAT CONTENT IN YOUR DIET

Food Category	Choose	Decrease
Meat Fish Poultry	• Lean cuts of meat with fat trimmed, such as: beef-round, sirloin, rump steak, loin • Poultry without skin • Pork tenderloin	• "Prime" grade meats • Fatty cuts, like: corned beef, brisket, short ribs, spareribs • Goose, duck, organ meats, sausage, bacon, hot dogs, regular luncheon meats
Dairy Products	• Skim milk. Lowfat buttermilk, lowfat evaporated or nonfat milk • Lowfat or non fat yogurts and cheeses	• Whole milk, cream, half & half, nondairy creamers, real or nondairy whipped cream, cream cheese, sour cream, ice cream custard-style yogurt • High-fat cheese, like Brie, Swiss, American, or Cheddar
Eggs	• Egg whites, cholesterol and fat-free egg substitutes	• Egg yolks (substitute 2 egg whites for 1 egg)
Fats Oils	• Unsaturated vegetable oils (in limited quantities): corn, olive, peanut, canola, safflower, sesame, soybean • Fat-free mayonnaise, cream cheese, and salad dressings • Mustard and flavored vinegars (when cooking, use spray oils or nonstick pans and decrease amount of fat in recipe by $1/3$ or substitute applesauce for fat)	• Butter, coconut oil, palm kernel oil, palm oil, lard, bacon fat

Breads Cereals Pasta	• Breads like whole wheat, pumpernickel, rye, pita, bagels, English muffins, rice cakes • Lowfat crackers and bread sticks • Plain cereals (hot and cold) • Spaghetti and macaroni • Any grain • Dried peas and beans	• Croissants, butter rolls, sweet rolls, pastries, doughnuts, most snack crackers, granola-type cereals made with saturated fats, egg noodles, pasta and rice prepared with cream, butter, or cheese sauces.
Vegetables Fruits	• Fresh, frozen, canned (no salt added)	• Vegetables prepared in butter, cream, or sauce • Fruits served in glazes

TEMPERATURE TESTS FOR CANDY MAKING

There are two different methods of determining when candy has been cooked to the proper consistency. One is by using a candy thermometer in order to record degrees; the other is by using the cold water test. The cart below will prove useful in helping to follow candy recipes:

TYPE OF CANDY	DEGREES	COLD WATER
Fondant, Fudge	234–238°	Soft Ball
Divinity, Caramels	245–248°	Firm Ball
Taffy	265–270°	Hard Ball
Butterscotch	275–280°	Light Crack
Peanut Brittle	285–290°	Hard Crack
Caramelized Sugar	310–312°	Caramelized

In using the **Cold-Water Test**, use a fresh cupful of cold water for each test. When testing, remove the candy from the fire and pour about _ teaspoon of candy into the cold water. Pick the candy up in the fingers and roll into a ball if possible.

In the **Soft Ball Test**, the candy will roll into a soft ball, which quickly loses its shape when removed from the water.

In the **Firm Ball Test,** the candy will roll into a firm, but not hard ball. It will flatten out a few minutes after being removed from the water.

In the **Hard Ball Test,** the candy will roll into a hard ball, which has lost almost all plasticity and will roll around on a plate on removal from the water.

In the **Light Crack Test**, the candy will form brittle threads, which will soften on removal from the water.

In the **Hard Crack Test,** the candy will form brittle threads in the water, which will remain brittle after being removed from the water.

In **Caramelizing**, the sugar first melts than becomes a gold brown. It will form a hard brittle ball in cold water.

UNDERSTANDING THE NUTRITION FACTS FOOD LABEL

The Nutrition Facts food label is designed to help the consumer make nutritious choices when selecting foods. It can be found on most packaged products in the grocery store. Information about serving size, calories, and several nutrients help to give an overall picture of the nutritional qualities of each food. The label on the following page is a typical example, although some labels list additional nutrients.

Serving Sizes have been set at an amount that people would typically eat. If your normal serving is smaller or larger, adjust the nutrient values accordingly. Serving sizes are in standard household and metric measures. Metric abbreviations used on the label include:

g: grams (28g = 1 ounce)
mg: milligrams (1,000mg = 1g)
ml: milliliters (30ml = 1 fluid ounce)

Nutrients listed are those considered to be important to today's health conscious consumer. These include total fat, saturated fat, cholesterol, sodium, and fiber.

The Percent of Daily Value tells you if the food is high or low in a particular nutrient. It also shows how that food fits into an entire day's diet. Percent of Daily Values are based on a 2,000-calorie diet and on current dietary guidelines. An individual's daily values may be higher or lower depending

continued on the next page

on calorie needs. As a rule of thumb, if the Dailey Value is 5% or less, the food contains only a small amount of that nutrient. For total fat, saturated fat, cholesterol, and sodium, foods with a low Percent of Daily Value are good choices.

Terms used on the label to describe the food's nutritional content have strict definitions set by the government. Eleven Descriptive Terms have been identified: free, low, lean, extra lean, less, reduced, light, fewer, high, more, and good source. Because precise guidelines must be met for a food to use one of these terms, you can be assured that the claim is believable. For example, if a food claims to be sodium free, it must have less than 5ml of sodium per serving.

Claims regarding a food's relationship to various health-related conditions must also meet specific guidelines. To make a health claim about fats and heart disease, a food must be low in total fat, saturated fat, and cholesterol. A food making a statement regarding blood pressure and sodium must be low in sodium.

The Ingredients List is located in a separate location on the label. Ingredients are listed in descending order by weight; thus, if the first ingredient is sugar, there is more sugar in that product than anything else.

See the following page for an example of the Nutritional Facts Food Label.

Nutrition Facts

Serving Size 1 cup (228g)
Servings Per Container 2

Amount Per Serving

Calories 250   Calories from Fat 110

	% Daily Value*
Total Fat 12g	**18%**
Saturated Fat 3g	**15%**
Trans Fat 3g	
Cholesterol 30mg	**10%**
Sodium 470mg	**20%**
Total Carbohydrate 31g	**10%**
Dietary Fiber 0g	**0%**
Sugars 5g	
Protein 5g	

Vitamin A	**4%**
Vitamin C	**2%**
Calcium	**20%**
Iron	**4%**

* Percent Daily Values are based on a 2,000 calorie diet.
Your Daily Values may be higher or lower depending on
your calorie needs.

	Calories:	2,000	2,500
Total Fat	Less than	65g	80g
Sat Fat	Less than	20g	25g
Cholesterol	Less than	300mg	300mg
Sodium	Less than	2,400mg	2,400mg
Total Carbohydrate		300g	375g
Dietary Fiber		25g	30g

FOOD PYRAMID

GRAINS | VEGETABLES | FRUITS | MILK | MEAT & BEANS

BEEF

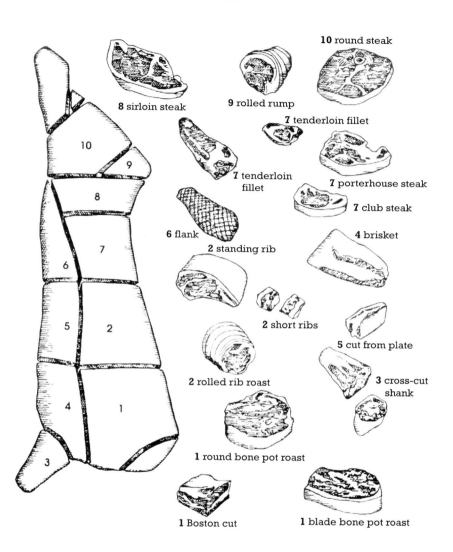

10 round steak

8 sirloin steak

9 rolled rump

7 tenderloin fillet

7 tenderloin fillet

7 porterhouse steak

7 club steak

6 flank

2 standing rib

4 brisket

2 short ribs

5 cut from plate

2 rolled rib roast

3 cross-cut shank

1 round bone pot roast

1 Boston cut

1 blade bone pot roast

PORK

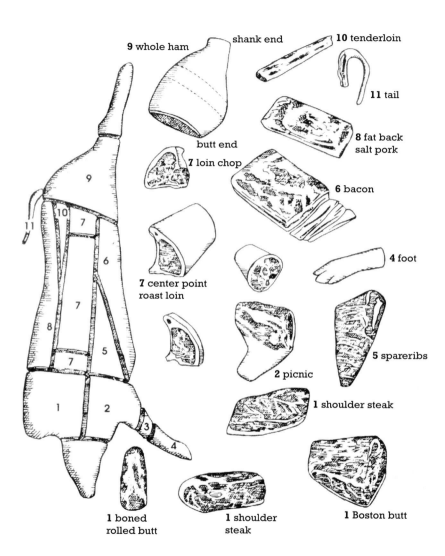

9 whole ham

shank end

10 tenderloin

11 tail

butt end

7 loin chop

8 fat back
salt pork

6 bacon

7 center point
roast loin

4 foot

5 spareribs

2 picnic

1 shoulder steak

1 boned
rolled butt

1 shoulder
steak

1 Boston butt

LAMB

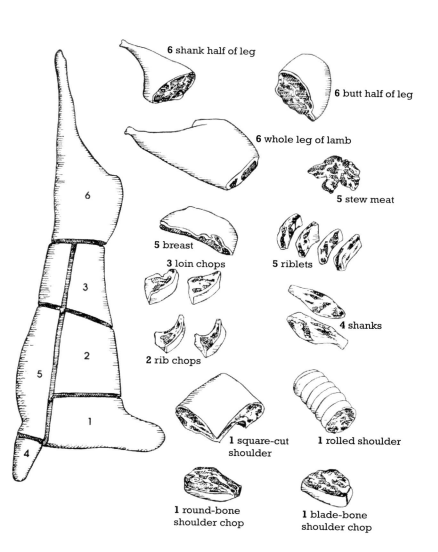

6 shank half of leg

6 butt half of leg

6 whole leg of lamb

5 stew meat

5 breast

5 riblets

3 loin chops

4 shanks

2 rib chops

1 square-cut shoulder

1 rolled shoulder

1 round-bone shoulder chop

1 blade-bone shoulder chop

VEAL

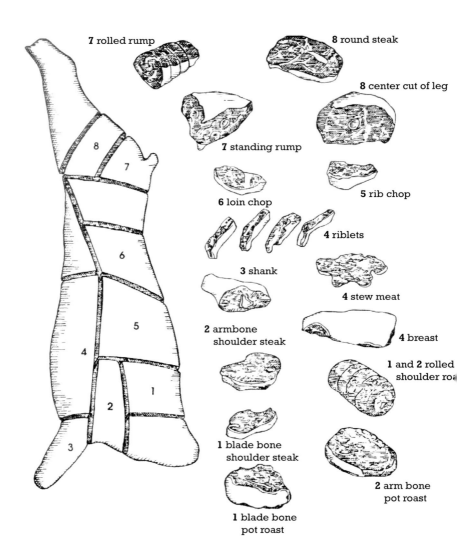

7 rolled rump

8 round steak

8 center cut of leg

7 standing rump

6 loin chop

5 rib chop

4 riblets

3 shank

4 stew meat

2 armbone shoulder steak

4 breast

1 and **2** rolled shoulder roa

1 blade bone shoulder steak

2 arm bone pot roast

1 blade bone pot roast

– 13 –

INDEX

NOTES

FAMOUS MOUNTAIN FOODS

APPETIZERS & BEVERAGES

BREADS

DESSERTS

MEAT

ASSEROLES

ALADS

SOUPS

VEGETABLES

BREAKFAST FOODS

ORDER FORM

For additional copies of this cookbook, please send check or money order payable to:

"It's the Real McCoy," Inc.
3337 Rushing Wind Lane
Lexington, KY 40511

I would like _____ copies of *Scratch Cooking 2* at $24.95 each, plus $3.50 postage and handling, sent to this address:

(Kentucky residents add 6% sales tax).

Name: _____

City: _____

State: _____ Zip: _____

You may order from my website at www.kentuckyscratchcooking.com.
Please allow 4 to 6 weeks for delivery.

....

ORDER FORM

For additional copies of this cookbook, please send check or money order payable to:

"It's the Real McCoy," Inc.
3337 Rushing Wind Lane
Lexington, KY 40511

I would like _____ copies of *Scratch Cooking 2* at $24.95 each, plus $3.50 postage and handling, sent to this address:

(Kentucky residents add 6% sales tax).

Name: _____

City: _____

State: _____ Zip: _____

You may order from my website at www.kentuckyscratchcooking.com.
Please allow 4 to 6 weeks for delivery.

My Favorite Kitchen Bouquet

She makes ginger-bread, corn-bread
Greasy beans and fried potatoes.
Cabbage cooked with ham hock
And fried green tomatoes—

Honey that's good country cookin!
As some of us old folks know it.
We even like the left-overs—
And some of us old folks show it...

She can do right fancy cookin too
Some things we have trouble spelling.
And she can take a little time out
To entertain with some story telling!

She has a smile for everyone,
"How's Miss Gennie today?"
"I haven't seen you in a coon's age,"
Sometimes you'll hear her say.

She is a "Real McCoy" alright
And likes giving herself away.
To somebody needing a little push
And so, she's our Kitchen Bouquet!

By Chester F. Powell